COPING
WITH
Longevity

A Family Journey With DEMENTIA *and* AGING

NICHOLAS TIMKO, JR.

outskirts
press

To all healthcare professionals who care for the elderly (Physicians, PAs, NPs, RNs, LPNs, CNAs), social workers, activities people, kitchen staff, support staff and all others who make life in *their world* a little better.

To my wife, Pat. Watching her work with the elderly for 30 years as a Registered Nurse (RN) showed me how it's done. Watching her work with her father in his world showed me she never forgot how it's done. She'll never stop being a nurse, and she's John's daughter to be sure. He still tells her "I love you" every time she's with him.

Acknowledgments

I'm indebted to all our family caregivers for remembering their stories, sharing their thoughts, and helping to make the photographs in this book complete. Without Mary, Pat, Rick, and Kathy, this book could not have been written.

Thanks also go to Marge for her constant words of wisdom regarding the care of John and Mary along their journey.

Table of Contents

Foreword

The focus of my care management practice for seventeen years has been helping elders age with the best quality of life possible, keeping as much independence as they are safely capable of maintaining. Given the many disjointed pieces of elder care, there is much to absorb and learn. With decisions to make; time constraints; and emotional, health and financial challenges, you may feel like you are on this path alone and wish to do nothing about it until a crisis occurs. It isn't uncommon for individuals and families to deny that help is needed, even with a recurring pattern of illness or memory loss. Families feel discomfort regarding the first steps of helping to share control with a parent who both fears the loss of independence and resists change. Rigidity and resistance to change puts elders and family caregivers in jeopardy and all too often propels them into the actual scenario they are fiercely trying to avoid.

In this book, the author invites the reader to come inside, get to know John and Mary Sedlak and follow their involuntary entry into the long-term care system. As the primary caregiver for her husband, Mary's health became compromised. Her adult children and their spouses provided a variety of support and were available without fail at a moment's notice to help. The family asked me to assess their parents' growing needs and provide some solutions for this final stage of their lives. In spite of her exhaustion and her own health problems, Mary was reluctant to accept any recommendations, expecting her family to continue to stay the course. Without the extraordinary family involvement, a crisis would have happened much sooner than it indeed did.

This book shares the uncertainties and small triumphs that go along with long-term care, as well as the blessings of having intact family nearby, which has become more of a rarity these days. People generally voice fear at the idea of allowing hired caregivers into their home or "going to a nursing home." I have consistently witnessed the surprised relief of elders and their families, as their frustrations and insistence on doing everything themselves wanes. We are now living very long lives. It is not realistic to believe you can live out your life without assistance of some kind from another person; however, help is available when you find the courage to seek it.

Marjorie Tubbert CMC, CDP

Preface

My wishes for this book are simple. If it helps one family or family friend dealing with dementia or Alzheimer's disease handle their situation a little better than they otherwise would have, then it will have made my writing effort worthwhile.

If it helps anyone reading it become more aware of what can happen to them or their friends or relatives as they travel their own life journeys, and if that increased awareness helps them to better handle what comes their way, then writing this story was worthwhile.

Finally, a few words to the healthcare professionals to whom this book is dedicated.

Somewhere between the time when you began your studies and eventually graduated, you changed. You changed because you learned that both medical and people skills are required to make a truly exceptional healthcare professional. If they're able to share their story, listening to your patients is a necessary part of helping you learn what makes them who they are. Those that master how to really listen to their patients become truly exceptional people. I hope this book inspires those healthcare professionals who read it to become exceptional people.

"You are in this profession as a calling, not a business; as a calling which exacts from you at every turn self-sacrifice, devotion, love and tenderness to your fellow-men. Once you get down to a purely business level, your influence is gone and the true light of your life is dimmed.

"Listen to your patient; he is telling you the diagnosis."

Quotes from Sir William Osler, a Canadian physician and one of the four founding professors of Johns Hopkins Hospital. He has been called the "Father of modern medicine."

Introduction

The idea for this book had been brewing in my mind for at least five years prior to my writing it. When I saw what dementia was doing to my father-in-law and our entire family, I began jotting down notes of any little event that was out of the ordinary. Just small slips of paper at first. I put these slips of paper into a folder and kept it on one of my bookshelves. There were lulls between stories, but soon enough another strange event would occur that had me jotting it down on another slip of paper.

In December of 2016, as our family sat around the Christmas dinner table reminiscing about all we remembered and how much of it had now changed, I watched how hearing those stories took my mother-in-law from laughter to tears. I knew then that it was time to do something with those slips of paper other than just continue filling a folder. What you hold in your hands now are my "slips of paper," arranged to help you take our family journey with us.

Before you begin, you will need a brief description of our family to help you better understand your journey.

The book centers around my father-in-law, John, and his wife of 72 years, Mary. I'm married to their first child Patricia (Pat to me, Patty to her mom, and "just what I always wanted" to her father (his first words after seeing her born)). She was a Registered Nurse for over 30 years, most of it in geriatric care, before cancer cut short her nursing career. Their second child, Richard (Rick to everyone), is an electrical engineer who spent many years self-employed in audio-visual repair. He now works for the State University of New York - Binghamton. He's married to Kathy, who has artistic and design talents too numerous to mention, in addition to her organizational skills as an office manager.

Mary, Pat, myself, Rick, and Kathy are the family caregivers you will read about throughout our journey. Caregivers are an indispensable part of dealing with dementia, for without them, those suffering with this dreaded affliction are aimlessly adrift without any links to who they still are. People with dementia are on a continuous journey, slowly progressing deeper into *their world*. Caregivers are with them on that journey, if only by looking through a window that allows them to catch glimpses of *their world* and letting them know that they're nearby for them.

—∞—

"Books have a unique way of stopping time in a particular moment and saying: Let's not forget this."

- Dave Eggers, American writer, editor, and publisher

PART ONE

BEFORE THE STORM

CHAPTER 1

The Early Years

John Growing Up

THE WEATHER IN Binghamton, New York on Friday, June 22nd, 1923 was near 90 degrees. It was officially the first day of summer, and the entire eastern United States was in the midst of a hot and humid spell of weather. The newspapers were full of stories of people dying from the heat; some becoming prostrated, and some committing suicide. It would be almost a decade later before air conditioners first began to appear.

Prohibition began on January 16th, 1920, when the Eighteenth Amendment went into effect. During prohibition, the manufacture, transportation, import, export, and sale of alcoholic beverages were restricted or were illegal. Warren G. Harding was the U.S. President, and prohibition was in the headlines on June 22nd, 1923. The front pages of many American newspapers were reporting the seizure of all beverage liquors by Federal Prohibition agents as they boarded all incoming ships in all of the major harbors in the United States.

John was born in Binghamton on that first day of summer in 1923. Oddly enough, Mary's mother and John's mother happened to share the same hospital room on the day of their deliveries. John's mother asked Mary's mother what she was naming her son (a son that passed away as a toddler). She told her, "John," to which John's mother replied, "that's a nice name, I'll name my son John too." Now that is a story of fate if there ever was one. Two years later, Mary's mother had a baby girl, and named her Mary. She eventually married John, who was given his first name by Mary's mother.

John was the third of six children, three boys and three girls. Anastasia (Stasia) was the oldest, then came Milton (Milt), John, Josephine (Josie), Marion, and Ronald (Ronnie). John was just a small boy when the Great Depression began, so the family fell upon some very hard times. Since John was between his three sisters in age, he often took the blame for mishaps around the house, as they were quick to point to him for most everything bad that happened. John's mother was in charge of disciplining the kids. Guess who was the underdog? John! He was the one always getting hit with a wooden stick that his mother used to pick clothes out of their wringer washing machine. When he first met

Mary, he cried as he told her of his beatings as a young-ster. He was so upset with it all that he planned to run away and join the Navy, but that never came about.

John always liked animals and very much wanted a dog for a pet, but his parents wouldn't allow it. Instead, John was given a pet guinea hen. He would feed his guinea hen before school, then couldn't wait to return home later in the day to spend more time with it. One day when he came home from school, his pet guinea hen was nowhere to be found. John searched every square foot of property around their house and the immediate neighborhood, but no guinea hen. He returned from his neighborhood search to have supper, and found his pet guinea hen being served! John knew that times were very hard in the years following the Great Depression, but he was so heartbroken by what had happened that he just went to his room and cried the evening away.

It was July 8th, 1935; a hot summer day in Binghamton. People on the street had heard that the Susquehanna River was cresting after torrential rains. A severe flood would soon devastate the city, so when John went home he told his mother of the impending disaster. She didn't believe him and beat him with a leather strap for telling her such lies. A short time later the family was in a rowboat because of the flood. The flood of 1938 left eighteen people dead in Broome County and $1.6 million in damage.

When John was still in his teens his father remarried, which made the house even more crowded because of new sleeping arrangements for them all. He was given a small bed that was placed on the enclosed, but unheated back porch. It was winter, and John could not keep warm with the few blankets he was given, so not long after this new sleeping arrangement began, John dismantled his small bed and moved it into the basement next to the furnace. It was far from a real bedroom, but it was warm! Shortly after, he went to live with his sister, Stasia, and her new husband.

World War 2

John went as far as the 10th grade in school, but left in 1941 to work and help support the family. He worked at Endicott Johnson Shoe Company from 1941 to 1943. World War 2 had begun and John was drafted into the Army Air Corps at age 19. It was January 29, 1943; John left Binghamton for Fort Niagara, New York to begin basic training. He served with the 466th Bomb Group assigned to the 8th Army Air Force in Attlebridge, England. He sailed aboard the Queen Mary, both to England and back to the United States, a trip that took five days each way. The Queen Mary first set sail as a passenger liner in 1936, but was converted to a troop carrier after World War 2 began. Part of the conversion called for a new camouflaged grey color paint, earning it the nickname "the grey ghost." John was a member of the ground crew for the B-24 Liberator bombers that flew uncountable missions over Germany in 1944 and 1945. He cleaned the bombers after they returned from each mission, then readied them to fly out again. He was responsible for caring for the bodies and body parts of American soldiers killed in action, and readied the wounded for transport to receive medical help. John was an exemplary soldier, a marksman, and always had a kind word for everyone. He was honorably discharged from military service at the Separation Center in Sioux Falls, South Dakota on October 18th, 1945.

John in his Army Air Force uniform in 1943

After The War

While home on a 30-day furlough from England, John married Mary on Saturday July 21st, 1945, just before his discharge scheduled for October. It was a warm and sunny day with temperatures topping out at 83 degrees. Page four of the Binghamton Press newspaper that day carried the wedding details in an article titled "Mary Kesa Is Married To Soldier." The only jewelry she wore on her wedding day was a gift from John--a string of pearls. He met Mary several years before he joined the Army Air Force (more about that soon), and they corresponded throughout the war. After his discharge, Mary wanted John to apply for a job at IBM Corporation in nearby Endicott, New York, because they were hiring right after the war. He didn't want to apply because he felt that he didn't have enough education, so John went back to Endicott Johnson where he worked before he left for the war. He became a fireman, which involved inspection of factories to ensure fire safety.

John spoke his mind more after the war, and one of his later superiors at Endicott Johnson didn't like that. John was worried about Mary's mother having to stand on a concrete floor while doing the laundry in her basement, so he took a small piece of scrap rubber from the trash bin to place it on the floor near her washing machine. This superior was informed that John took the scrap rubber, and immediately he drummed up a charge of stealing. Mary went with John to see the Endicott Johnson CEO, Frank Johnson, who saw the pettiness of the charge. He dismissed it and reinstated John. The value of the scrap piece of rubber was listed as $7.91.

After Endicott Johnson, John went to work for nearby St. Bernadette Hospital in Binghamton, where he worked as a security guard for a short time. After that, he worked for GAF Corporation briefly, then settled in working for Ozalid Corporation, where he was a paper machine operator for many years, making blue and brown line paper for large copiers. Blue lines and brown lines were copies commonly used by engineering firms during the 1960s and beyond.

Mary, Growing Up and Meeting John

Mary grew up with a younger sister. Mary was usually the one working hard helping her mother around the house and yard. Her younger sister managed to conveniently hide away when it was time for chores. Mary would wash windows, wash walls inside the house (yes, wash walls), and help with meals. Her mother seemed to blame Mary for whatever problems surfaced at home, and she was spanked many times. Many years later, she asked her mother why she never spanked her younger sister, to which her mother replied, "I always felt sorry for her."

Mary's father made her leave school after the 10th grade, telling her, "school poisons your mind." He took her to a perfume factory in Binghamton called Karlovas. The man who interviewed her told Mary's father, "this girl should not work, she belongs in school," but her father insisted that she work. So she did. After Karlovas, Mary found an office job at Remington Rand, then another office job at Endicott Johnson. After a short time, she went to the New York State Unemployment Office and met a woman who told her that her husband was the business agent for the local Bricklayer's Union, so she arranged for Mary to have an interview. That led to her opportunity as the office manager for the Bricklayer's Union for over twenty years.

When Mary was about fourteen years old, she met John for the first time. The parents of the two families knew each other and would often see each other at local summer picnics, where ethnic Slovak music was always a part of the entertainment. That Slovak music was to keep them dancing together for decades to come. John always loved his Slovak music, and would sing and dance every time he heard it played. (In his later years John sang these songs while taking his shower.) John seemed to always "hang around" Mary once they met, but Mary wasn't really interested in him. When Mary was about sixteen years old, John's family moved into a house very close to Mary's parents, so John continued to pursue Mary, as they were now neighbors.

John and Mary enjoying spring on April 26, 1942

Once John was drafted and sent to England for active duty during World War 2, they began writing letters to each other. John would often write about the hard life he had while growing up during the Depression. It was a difficult life for everyone, let alone a family as large as John's. Mary felt sorry for him, perhaps because she too was the one in her house who bore the brunt of much punishment whenever bad things happened.

John and Mary's Wedding Day, July 21, 1945

After they married in July of 1945, John returned to England until his discharge in October. They didn't have any money to speak of, so they lived with Mary's parents for several years until they scraped up enough money to put down on a house of their own in Johnson City. John's cousin lived nearby and John and Mary visited them often. They saw a nearby plot of land being readied for new home construction and decided to show it to Mary's parents, who liked the area so much that they bought a home that was near completion.

11

John and Mary liked the area too, so they eventually saved up $1,500 as a down payment on a house that only had a concrete foundation poured at the time. They continued to live with Mary's parents in their new home until their own home was completed. They finally bought their first and only home in 1948. It had a price of $8,400, and their mortgage was $48 per month. The backyard of John and Mary's home adjoined with the backyard of her parents' new home, so they spent many hours over the years just enjoying being together beneath the trees and lilacs they planted.

L to R: Mary's Dad, Mom, Patty, Mary, c. 1952

———∝∝———

"We are not rich by what we possess but by what we can do without."

- *Immanuel Kent, 18th century philosopher*

CHAPTER 2

Stories of John Before Dementia

MY FATHER-IN-LAW, JOHN, is an interesting guy. Seldom was there a boring visit with him. This chapter contains some of the most memorable stories I have of him. We first met in 1969, and I shared many good times with him as a member of the family.

The Handy, Candy Man Can

John was a handyman around the house, always trying to fix or repair something that wasn't working correctly, whether it was a drain in a sink, a toilet, or his lawn mower. He enjoyed being outdoors in his yard; mowing, tending to a small raised bed garden full of tomato and onion plants, or just sitting on a swing beneath his birch trees—relaxing. He also enjoyed just taking a stroll through the woods and enjoying nature.

One day when John was working in his basement cutting some wood on his circular table saw, he accidentally happened to slice off the tip of one of his fingers as he moved a piece of wood through the cutting blade. He was home alone at the time, but managed to find the small tip in the pile of wood chips on the floor, and wrapped both the tip and the rest of his bleeding finger in a handkerchief. He walked out to his car and drove himself to the emergency room at Staunton General Hospital, only a few miles away. He walked into the emergency room with his hand wrapped in the handkerchief and went to the check-in desk. The woman in charge asked him what the problem was. John replied, "You people are the doctors, you tell me," as he simultaneously unwrapped his finger, allowing the small tip to fall on the countertop along with his bloodied handkerchief. The woman became quite dizzy, but by all reports she did not pass out. John always did have a bit of a flair for the dramatic.

As for candy, John loved fireballs (also known as fireball jawbreakers) and would always have a shirt pocket full of them to munch on. In the summer he usually wore a t-shirt with a pocket so that his fireballs were always handy. He wore a full set of dentures by middle age, so the clicking of his teeth while chewing fireballs drove all of us crazy in a laughable sort of way.

Take Me Out to the Ballgames

John was a baseball fan. His favorite team was the New York Mets, but he always had stories to tell about great players from other teams; two of his favorites were Babe Ruth and Yogi Berra. During the 1980s I took John and my father (also a baseball fan) to Yankee Stadium to see the New York Yankees play, and also several visits to Shea Stadium to see the New York Mets.

Back in the early 1970s when Pat and I were first married, several of my longtime friends and I got together to form a softball team to play against similar teams in our community. I made up nice t-shirts with each player's name and number on the back, and the team-name in big letters on the front—*The Johnson City Polaks*. We actually had a really good team that summer. Our star pitcher, and oldest team member—was John. He smoked cigarettes back then, so the guys nicknamed him "Smoky John." He had one helluva drop ball. Can't you just see a grey-haired man in his 50s, with a cigarette hanging off his lower lip, striking out guys less than half his age?

It was Cap Day at Shea Stadium on Sunday, the 12th of June, 1983. I took my father and John to New York City to see future hall of famer, Tom Seaver, pitch. We arrived early so not many players were even on the field warming up yet, but one guy was doing wind sprints and working up quite a sweat. You guessed it, Tom Seaver. The Mets were playing the Montreal Expos that day and we got to see another future hall of famer play too. Gary Carter was then the catcher for Montreal. Seaver pitched the entire game—a 4-hitter as the Mets downed Montreal 9 to 1. John and my father were like kids again. They loved it, although John, being fair-skinned, endured quite a sunburn on his face and arms. After all, it was a hot, sunny day, and we sat in the sun on the third base side all afternoon.

On a warm, but cloudy day in August of 1986 I drove John and my father to Doubleday Field in Cooperstown, New York to see the annual Hall of Fame game. It was an 85 mile ride from home. Doubleday Field, which seats nearly 10,000 fans, was named after Abner Doubleday, a major general in the Civil War. He was historically credited with inventing the game of baseball. Babe Ruth played at the first Hall of Fame game in Cooperstown in 1939. John always reminded me of that. The Cooperstown residents who lived near the field made their lawns available for automobile parking for the fans, which made for a shorter walk for those who came early enough to find a lawn to park on. It was a packed house to see this historic game--the first time that two teams from the same league played one another in a Hall of Fame game.

John and Babe Ruth, Hall of Fame, June 1991

The Texas Rangers were the home team that afternoon. Early in the game, 22-year-old rookie Texas outfielder, Pete Incaviglia, drove a hard line drive down the left field line that was still climbing as it cleared the fence for a home run. We were close enough to hear the whoosh of the ball as it flew past us. John and my father both went wild! John yelled out "POW! Did you see that swing?"

John liked that word POW; he used it all the time. Future hall of famer, George Brett, played third base for the Kansas City Royals that afternoon. He hit a home run in the fourth inning, but it wasn't enough, as the Texas Rangers came out on top 11 to 4. John talked about that game for many years, and always remembered all of the baseball hall of fame players that he saw play throughout the years.

———✕✕○———

"Always go to other people's funerals, otherwise they won't go to yours."

Yankee hall of famer Yogi Berra
(John always laughed when he told me this, along with many other Yogi-isms.)

———✕✕○———

California Here We Come

John is one of the most relaxed men I know. He could always take a nap in the middle of doing anything, without hesitation. I tell you this fact because of what the California trip he and I took in August of 1984 had in store for us.

John wanted to see his older sister, Anastasia, that summer, as she was nearing her 70th birthday soon. Anastasia was the oldest sister in the family, about eight years older than John. She and her husband, John, lived in Hemet, California, in the desert east of Los Angeles. I planned a week-long trip to California for John and me that included a visit to see his sister, spending some time seeing the sights in the Los Angeles area, then driving to San Francisco to see the sights before flying home. After visiting his sister, taking in Universal Studios, walking through the Queen Mary (the very ship John sailed both to and from England during World War 2), and seeing a Los Angeles Dodgers evening baseball game, we set out early one morning to make the 400-mile, 7-hour ride north to San Francisco.

John aboard the Queen Mary 40 years later, August 1984

We got an early start as we knew it was going to be a long day. I drove through Los Angeles on Route 5, and the morning traffic was the usual bumper to bumper, multi-lane variety for which the city is famous. Once north of the city limits I let John take over the driving, and we enjoyed the beautiful scenery along the way. I had to make one stop at an engineering firm near Bakersfield, as I was working on a project with them related to my job as a mechanical engineer at the IBM Corporation. We weren't too far from Bakersfield when I suddenly noticed that John was veering off the road. As I glanced at him, I saw that he had fallen asleep! I quickly grabbed the steering wheel and began to maneuver the rental car back onto the highway, as we were already completely on the shoulder of the highway and headed for the gravel-filled ditch be-yond. John, now startled awake by my grabbing the steering wheel, started screaming, "What are you do-ing, what are you doing?"

"You're going off the road, slow down," I yelled. Between John pumping the brakes and me steering us back onto the pavement, we managed to avoid a major accident that day. A rest area was just ahead, so we pulled off. John got out of the car and started walk-ing around the grassy area beyond the parking spaces, swinging both arms in a huge windmill-like circular motion. I knew the definition of tachycardia (rapid heartbeat), but in those early moments following the mishap, I became a poster boy for what tachycardia "looks like." I had an ashen complexion, sweaty face, and the shirt covering my chest bounced up and down like a bongo player's hands.

From that day forward, I always kept one eye open whenever John was driving.

The Music Man Wannabe

John's Slovak heritage was in his blood, especially their music in all its forms. He especially loved the brass band music of Czechoslovakia and Germany, and would play it quite often on his stereo in his living room. John became hard of hearing as time went on, so he played his beloved music quite loud; partly to compensate for his hearing loss, and partly because he just loved to hear it. There was many a day when I would stop by to visit, and as I parked the car and stopped the engine, I would hear him blasting his music as if I were standing next to him. And that was with all the doors and windows of the house closed! It wasn't unusual to see the mailman making a delivery on their front porch literally bouncing about from the vibration of the front porch floor as he tried to stand still long enough to place the mail in the mailbox.

John never learned how to play an instrument, but that didn't stop him. He bought a used tuba at a second hand store, polished it nicely, and "played" that tuba quite often. He didn't know how to read music at all, or how to finger the tuba to create actual notes, but his pattern of toots was always right in time with the music he loved so much.

John and Mary's 50th Anniversary, July 1995

He had an exhaustive collection of long playing ethnic Slovak and Czech records, and as time went on he
created cassette tapes of many of them to play, either
in his car, or in a small cassette tape player that he
took with him when he wished to enjoy his music in
a place other than his living room. He spent countless
hours in his basement "studio" recording and playing
his collection of cassette tapes.

John in his basement studio, July 2001

In September of 1989 I took my father and John to what was then still communist Czechoslovakia, for a two week trip to see the sights and visit relatives. Music was a big part of that trip and John enjoyed it so much that he went back several more times by himself.

John's favorite Czech song was written by Czech composer, Jaromir Vejvoda. Vejvoda wrote the world famous "Beer Barrel Polka" in 1927, and wrote John's favorite "Kde Jsi Mé Mládí Valčík" ("Where Are Those Days Of My Youth Waltz") in 1938. The words are

25

quite appropriate for this book, as they underscore precisely what many people feel as they get older. Some of the lyrics to the song (translated) are:

"Where they've gone, those carefree days of my youth, gone away, and never to return.........Oh so happy, I tell you now the truth, and for'er my love, remember youth"

Peony Park

John's intense, long-lasting love of his ethnic music led me to book an airline flight for the two of us to Omaha, Nebraska in September of 1974. There are a large number of Czech people in the Midwest of the United States, and Omaha is a typical region that not only celebrated, but was also a recording center for Czech and Slovak music. Every year Omaha holds a festival called the Nebraska Polka Days, held at Peony Park. It lasts for three or four days, with almost nonstop music from morning until night, simultaneously being played on multiple stages throughout the park.

When we arrived at Eppley Airfield in Omaha, I rented a car and drove John and myself to the motel we'd occupy for the next several days. On our way to the motel, John said that he was hungry and wanted a McDonald's ® hamburger. Now, a hamburger in Omaha tastes like no other, since it was probably slaughtered only hours, or a day or two before grilling it. As we stood in line John decided to order a children's McDonald's Happy Meal®! I looked at him in amazement, but knowing him, I decided to just let it go and see what happens. His meal came in a small cardboard box designed like a choo-choo train, and contained a hamburger, French fries, and a cookie. Also included was a small prize; in this case, a small tub of playdough. John loved the hamburger, and played with the play dough all the while we were in Omaha.

The music at the park was phenomenal. Since I played drums in several ethnic bands at the time, I could see the real talent that so many of these bands possessed. We got to meet several of the musicians who played and recorded the records that John already owned, so meeting them was a special thrill. They befriended us and took us to their recording studio, which left John speechless. We were invited to the Saturday night dance at the Sokol Hall in Omaha where they performed. John danced away that entire trip, both at Peony Park and at the Sokol Hall. He enjoyed that trip so much that we went back for another visit in September of 1976.

John with Nebraska Czech recording star
Al Grebnick, May 1996

Quiet! Hitler Needs a Hearing Aid

When I returned to college to study for a second career in dental hygiene, I spent a great deal of time at the college library, doing research for my dental studies and also tutoring a microbiology course. John was a World War 2 history buff, so I decided to take him with me to the college library one Saturday to let him browse through the books available on World War 2. John was already hard of hearing in the mid-1990s but had not yet been fitted for hearing aids, so I had to get my lips right next to his ear so that I didn't disturb everyone in the library while I gave him directions on where to locate the World War 2 books he wanted to see. As he was browsing through the books I took a seat at a nearby study booth. Being a Saturday, nearly all of the study booths throughout the entire library were filled with students doing their homework.

John was really enjoying browsing. I could tell because he was humming some of his favorite Slovak songs—so loud that I had to tell him to try and keep his voice down because we had to be quiet in a library.

He smiled and said, "OK," but soon after, his humming continued. He then surprised me as he stopped humming his Slovak songs and began humming the "Colonel Bogey March." A short time later as I was again engrossed in my research, John walked over to me and blurted in a voice much too loud for a library atmosphere, "Did you know that Hitler only had one ball?"

As I sank into my seat trying to hide my embarrassment, most of the students in nearby booths began laughing uncontrollably, and John right along with them. One of the guys came over, so John immediately struck up a conversation with him. It turned out that he happened to be a history buff himself, so he and John went outside and talked about John's experiences in World War 2.

John could always talk with most anyone at the drop of a hat, and that Saturday afternoon was no exception. With him it was as simple as beginning a discussion with a complete stranger about Hitler's undescended right testicle.

"Hitler Has Only Got One Ball" was a popular 1939 British song that mocked Nazi leaders. It was sung to the tune of the "Colonel Bogey March." John remembered all of the men in his Attlebridge, England air base singing it as they readied their B-24 airplanes for a bombing mission.

> *Göring has only got one ball,*
> *Hitler's [are] so very small,*
> *Himmler's so very similar,*
> *And Goebbels has no balls at all.*

CHAPTER **3**

The Family Remembers John Before Dementia

Mary Remembers

MY JOHN WAS always a good guy. He took a liking to me and my parents from the very beginning. When he came home from the Army on furlough, duffel bag and all, where did he go? Not to his parents. He came to see me and my parents at our house, and they accepted him.

Later, when we were already married, I remember that John always liked working nights. Early in our marriage, money was scarce for us. I recall sitting in one corner of the kitchen floor and crying because we had no money for groceries. My mother (Justina) and father (Frank) lived just around the corner from us at

31

that time (now Kathy and Rick's house), so they often stopped over to see how things were going. My mother caught me crying, and later that same day she and my father brought us several bags of groceries. When they heard that John and I were sleeping on the floor because we couldn't afford any bedroom furniture, they bought us a new bedroom set. The first draperies on our windows were paper drapes! Philadelphia Sales, a local, inexpensive general merchandise and department store, sold them. They were all we could afford at the time. Times were very hard for us during those early years together.

As good a guy as John was, he was never adept at budgeting or saving money. Even when he was in the Army, he never saved any of his money; he just blew it on different things from week to week. When John was working at Endicott Johnson Shoe Corporation, he needed to take on a part time job bagging groceries at a P&C Supermarket so we would have enough money to buy groceries for ourselves.

Because the money issue was such a big part of those early years, I was often mean to John. I was always the one in charge of budgeting the money. I had envelopes for everything; but the mortgage, electric, gas and water bills, and money for taxes took so much of what he brought home that the grocery money envelope was often empty. After a while, I decided that

I too had to go to work to help us make ends meet. By then we had Patty, so I looked for a part time job that gave me early evening hours (5:00 to 8:00 PM), when John was at home. I found such a job at the Philadelphia Sales store. I straightened out display counters, folded clothes on display, and worked the cash register.

Around that time, John decided on his own to buy a new car—a 1950 Hudson. When I came home and saw that car, I exploded. "How are we going to pay for it?" I screamed.

John had taken out a loan of some sort, adding to our ever present monetary woes. Soon after, I left Philadelphia Sales for a job doing collating at a local printing company because they gave me an extra hour to work. I worked there from 5:00 to 9:00 PM.

It wasn't until the mid-1960s, when both Patty and her brother Rick were old enough to be left alone for a while, that I found a job as the business office manager for the Bricklayer's Union. It was a full time position, but I felt that it was necessary in order to have enough money to cover all of our needs. I anticipated college for both of our kids, so we had to start saving for that too.

Yes, John was always a good guy. Through all my

complaining and screaming over the years, he never raised a hand towards me. He was who he was, and he never complained—never.

———∞———

"What a weary time those years were -- to have the desire and the need to live but not the ability."

- Charles Bukowski, German-born American author, from his book Ham on Rye. (Bukowski was the only child of an American soldier and a German mother.)

———∞———

Pat Remembers

I always remember how I loved to cuddle up with my father in his chair when I was a little girl. He was easy to cuddle with.

My father told us stories of his time working at St. Bernadette Hospital as a security guard. He would be called to a floor when a patient had passed away, and wheel the body to the morgue. Whenever a patient escaped from the hospital he would be sent out looking for him or her.

I remember how he always took care of my grandmother's property. He would mow the lawn, shovel the snow, and fix whatever needed repair around her house. He really took care of two houses for many years, and never once complained.

When I was a teenager I remember my father being a chain smoker. He and the neighbor across the street used to stand outside on warm summer days and just talk and smoke. Both of them would light the next cigarette with the one between their lips, ready to burn out. I knew that wasn't healthy for either of them.

My father would always help any of us that needed it. He would drop whatever he was doing to help out. When we moved to our newly built house in 1986, I can't even count how many carloads of boxes and clothes he moved for us. He spent countless hours just packing his car with boxes, then unpacking them at our new house.

One summer day soon after we had become the owners of our white West Highland Terrier, Andy, John was watching him for us. He loved to take Andy for walks, and they had just returned from one in the nearby woods. Every time John came to our house to take him, Andy would run like lightning for the door, tail wagging full force, waiting to go! John was just as excited as Andy, usually telling him, "OK, let's go pal!"

On this day, John was in the kitchen making coffee to have with his lunch of macaroni and cheese, already on his plate on the nearby back porch table. In the minute or so that it took for John to get his coffee ready, Andy had jumped up onto the couch next to the table, and like a pogo stick he sprang up onto the back porch table chair, devouring all of John's macaroni and cheese before John even knew what happened. As John walked out on the porch, he saw Andy's innocent looking face, with his whiskers now all smeared with red tomato sauce and yellow cheese, and he just laughed and laughed.

Some years back, there was an incident that involved my father and a family friend who happened to have the same name, John Sedlak. How St. Bernadette Hospital got the two mixed up one day remains a mystery, as they had different birth dates. The hospital called my father to come to the hospital for a physician-ordered CT scan intended for the "other" John Sedlak. My father had the CT scan and told us he really enjoyed it. He said it was relaxing. The staff loved him, as he slept through most of it. When my father's physician received the test results, he quickly saw to it that my father and his health insurance weren't paying for an obvious hospital error. The only finding on his mistakenly-taken CT scan was a long standing broken rib that ironically happened when he fell off a ladder while working as a security guard for St. Bernadette Hospital years before.

Not long before we all began to see the changes of dementia taking hold of my father, he and my mom were at home one morning getting ready to have breakfast. Mom had recently had cataract surgery done on her eyes and was told to wear sunglasses for a while. She did just that, including wearing them in the house! My father was already in the kitchen making his breakfast, and Mom was just coming down the stairs from their second floor, sunglasses on, sliding on her behind so as to minimize aggravating her painful right knee. As she neared the last step, she suddenly fell onto the floor. She let out a very loud yell for my father to come and help her because she had fallen, unable to get up. My father heard her and yelled back, "I'll be there in a minute, my eggs aren't done yet!" So much for priorities.

"I suddenly remember being very little and being embraced by my father. I would try to put my arms around my father's waist, hug him back. I could never reach the whole way around the equator of his body; he was that much larger than life. Then one day, I could do it. I held him, instead of him holding me, and all I wanted at that moment was to have it back the other way."

- Jodi Picoult, bestselling American author, from her book Vanishing Acts

Rick Remembers

I remember arriving home after a family Florida vacation. My father was driving. When we pulled into our driveway, he had to get out of the car to open the garage door because we had no automatic door opener. He left the car in drive, so the car rolled forward and dented the garage. A 2,500 mile trip with no problems until we arrived in our driveway!

One day when I was just learning how to drive a car, I had to go to the store with my father. As he was driving, he came upon a stop sign, but he didn't come to a complete stop. I told him that we were being taught that you have to come to a complete stop at a stop sign. His reply was, "Rick, when you're my age, they don't care anymore." Now how do you argue with logic like that?

As my father was building our upstairs bedrooms and bathroom, it required cutting a lot of wood. I never knew why he hadn't brought his circular table saw up to the second floor as he did all this work, but he didn't. He left it in the basement. Every time he mismeasured he had to go back down to the basement to cut the piece again, swearing all the way down and back. He always wanted that saw, but Mom didn't think he needed it. They argued over that and didn't talk for days. I always thought that it was quite amazing that he had no training on how to build and finish rooms, but he did it all by himself. He lost quite a bit of weight during those months of constant running up and down the stairs every day.

When we bought a roof TV antenna, my father went on the roof to adjust it so as to receive a good picture. I was in the window relaying messages from my mom, who was watching the TV. I remember going back and forth, yelling, "better—worse—better." My father kept yelling, "Where the hell do you want it?"

We always exchanged Christmas gifts on Christmas Eve. One Christmas Mom bought my father a really nice sleeveless sweater vest. He opened it and said, "Where are the sleeves?" He looked it over for another minute; first one side, then the other. Then he just threw it on the floor and said, "Thanks anyway."

L to R: Me, Pat, Rick, Mary, Kathy, John, Christmas 1999

Kathy Remembers

I remember one summer when Pat and Mary had gone to the Amish country in Lancaster, Pennsylvania to spend a weekend. Mary called John to see how everything was at home, but he didn't answer, so she called me and asked if I could go over and check to see if everything was alright. As I walked over and got closer to their house, I began to hear some very loud Czech music. I walked onto their vibrating front porch and opened the front door, blocking my ears from the loud music. I yelled, "John! John!"

He didn't answer. He was having a grand old time standing in front of his stereo pretending to direct the musicians playing in the band! As I was behind him when I walked in, I went right up to his ear and yelled again, "John!" He finally heard me, turned to me, and simply said, "What?"

I remember that John wouldn't hesitate to set up a practical joke. After he was retired, he worked part time for a local florist delivering floral arrangements. He told me that when the manager of the flower shop was making an arrangement and the phone rang, she would have to answer it if no one else was in the shop at the time. John would be sitting in the shop waiting for an arrangement to be completed so he could deliver it. When the manager went into the next room to answer the phone, he would go outside and pick some dandelions and stick them in her arrangement. Sneaky guy!

CHAPTER 4

Early Signs of Dementia

Of Hearts and Nazis

JOHN WAS 83 years old in the summer of 2007. I was still playing my drums with several local bands that year. Whenever our ethnic brass band had a scheduled performance at a public event, John would usually go with me to sit and enjoy the music, since it was *his kind of music.* He had been seeing a cardiologist regularly at Staunton General Hospital, so the family thought that he was being adequately assessed and cared for. Our brass band had an evening performance at Westmoor Hall Nursing Home one warm November evening. As I pulled up next to the canopy covering Westmoor Hall's entry, John asked if he could help me carry in some of my drum equipment. He always asked. I gave him a few lightweight cases to carry in, one at a time; one small drum case,

41

and one small case with cymbal parts. As we walked down the hallway leading to the dining room where we were to set up and perform, I noticed that John was really out of breath. We hadn't walked but more than twenty-five steps from the car, and all those steps were on flat ground, so it really struck me that he was so severely out of breath. I asked him about it but he made a joke out of it as he usually did, so I let it go—for that evening.

The next day I called Oxana, a nurse practitioner I knew quite well who worked in cardiology at the Sarah Wright Clinic less than forty miles from home. I explained the story to her and asked if she could help us get an appointment at the Sarah Wright Clinic for a second opinion, as I found out that John's current cardiologist had essentially dismissed his shortness of breath issue as *old age*. (John was told to take it easy and he'll see him again in six months.) She said that she would see what she could do. She called me several hours later with an appointment for John to see the head of the Sarah Wright Clinic Cardiology Unit later that week!

When John met with the head of Cardiology at Sarah Wright; Mary, Pat, and I were with him. Dr. Livingston reviewed the tests that the Staunton General Cardiology Unit was asked to forward to him, but he also ran a few more tests that morning. After looking at all of the test information now before him, Dr. Livingston said to John, "You need your aortic valve replaced." John was quick to reply with, "What are you doing this afternoon?" Mary questioned such a procedure at John's age but Dr. Livingston explained that aortic valve replacement was regularly performed on people into their 90s with wonderful results.

Within a week, John was admitted to the hospital affiliated with and attached to the Sarah Wright Clinic; Franklin General, to have open heart surgery. John was his usual, jovial self as they wheeled him into the operating room that morning. Cardiothoracic surgeon Dr. Susan Ricardo performed the surgery, after which she met with us all to report on the results. She told us that the procedure went well; John now had a pig valve functioning within his heart.

John was in his room at Franklin General that night, but his heart was having a problem keeping his heart rate in the satisfactory range. It wasn't long before the doctors determined that he needed to have a pacemaker implanted, so Dr. Ricardo was again the surgeon called upon, this time to implant a pacemaker. It did the job and John's heart was functioning as it should.

During the time John spent in his room at Franklin General, he began to hallucinate. When I visited him one evening he told me to warn his son, Rick, before he comes to visit, because he's seeing Nazi tanks coming toward the hospital. The nurses told us that later that evening, John barricaded himself in his room by placing several chairs up against his room door. John had a properly functioning heart once again, but his concerns centered around, not his heart, but rather a Nazi invasion of the hospital! It's often been said that war can leave permanent scars upon those who served. John made me a believer, as almost 65 years had passed since he was stationed in England during World War 2.

In the months and years that followed, Pat would take John to the Sarah Wright Clinic for follow up exams and pacemaker checks. While driving down Route 71 to the clinic, John would always point to the radio towers as they passed by them along the way. He would say to Pat, "Do you see those towers? They're watching us." Was John still *seeing* Nazis trying to invade us? Once their visits at the clinic were finished, they would walk down the hallway leading to the elevators that took them to the cafeteria. While in the hallway, John would always remark, "Look at these floors—beautiful! This place is so clean." Once in the cafeteria, they would sit at a table where John had his coffee and doughnut and just enjoy the view. His words were always the same, "I really like this place."

———∞———

"War has many noticeable consequences, but it also takes a toll on the health and well-being of survivors over the course of their lives."

- Iris Kesternich, Ph.D., Munich University

———∞———

Memory Loss and Eventful Confusion

During the years following John's aortic valve surgery, we noticed a gradual tendency for him to become more easily confused; subtle at first, but more obvious as time went on. He would deflect the issue and joke about it as he often did about most things. One of the earliest signs of dementia happened most every morning when John came downstairs without wearing his dentures. Mary would always ask, "John, did you forget something?" As principal caregiver, Mary tried to dismiss his confusion as just old age at first. She's a proud woman, a motivated achiever as one engineer friend of mine labeled her after first meeting her many years ago, but even the strongest of us will eventually wear down from the daily added stress of giving ever-increasing levels of care to a loved one.

John still loved to walk around his neighborhood block when the weather was nice. He also really enjoyed just sitting on a chair on his front porch and simply watching nothing in particular. He would spend hours doing that. One day after John had just taken one of his strolls around the block, he told Mary that he was going upstairs to do something. After about ten minutes, Mary crawled upstairs on her hands and knees to check on him, but John was no longer there. She hurried down the stairs as best she could, sliding down on her behind, and flew out the door hobbling in pain as she got into her car and went looking for him. A neighbor saw her frenzied state and told her that he happened to see John in the used car lot a block away on the main road, so Mary hurriedly drove there. Sure enough there was John, standing in front of a used car and talking to a salesman. Mary asked John what he was doing, and he replied, "I'm looking for a new car!" Mary took John by the hand, apologized to the salesman, and they returned home.

Several months later, Mary had to help out at a bake sale being held at their church, so Pat and I took John out for breakfast. It was our turn to be caregivers for several hours. As we looked over our menus to decide what to order, the waitress asked John what he would like. He looked at Pat, smiled, and said, "You know what I like." He wasn't able to remember what he liked to eat, and the menu choices only confused him. He could read the words, but that didn't help him make any decisions. So Pat ordered his favorite breakfast: two eggs over easy, home fries, white bread toast, and coffee (with four packets of sugar). As we were eating, John kept talking about his wife being scheduled to have an operation on her rear end soon! He seldom called Mary by her name now, but he was absolutely convinced that she was going to the hospital soon to have this operation. Of course, no such procedure had been planned, but we got a good laugh out of his story.

John and Mary's next door neighbor, Steve, was retired. He enjoyed working in his yard, so he could easily see what John was doing if they were both outside. One summer day, Steve was taking a walk around the block as John also enjoyed doing. As he walked by a house on the far side of the block, he spotted John inside the garage at that home. He walked down the driveway and asked John what he was doing. John replied that he was just looking around at the things in the garage. Steve nicely talked with John as he suggested that they both leave and finish their walk—which they did. John had lost the concept of his vs. other people's property.

When Pat drove John to various appointments, he would often repeat a story that never did make much sense. He would always tell her about the time he was discharged from the Army Air Force and came home from England. He took a train home and told her that there was no one on that train but himself. He had the entire train to himself, and he really enjoyed it!

"Time's the thief of memory"

- Stephen King, author,
from "The Gunslinger"

Forgetting and Falling – The Devil Made Me Do It

John never lost his love for Czech and Slovak music, but he gradually began to have a harder time remembering how to use his stereo equipment. He could still place an LP record on the turntable, but had trouble remembering how to turn on everything needed to make it work. If he was trying to play a CD in the attached CD player, he wouldn't remember how to insert the CD. Writing directions out for him didn't help. He could read them, but he could not interpret what the words were telling him to do. After a while, John began to leave the stereo on after he finished listening to his music. He no longer remembered to turn it off.

I would find CDs that he had listened to either not in their proper cases, loosely strewn about, or placed in the wrong case. He was no longer able to match the CD to its case even if the names or pictures on both were the same.

John loved to watch stories about World War 2 on television. He enjoyed watching any program that depicted the life and times of German Chancellor Adolf Hitler. Even though John left England and World War 2 in 1945, his mind could always return to that time in an instant. It wasn't at all surprising then that one of his favorite television shows was *Hogan's Heroes*, a comedic spoof about a group of allied prisoners living in a German prisoner of war camp during World War 2; run by a goofy, bumbling commandant and his equally goofy officers. John would laugh uncontrollably as he watched the antics in every episode. One Christmas I gave John a DVD collection of *Hogan's Heroes* episodes that he would watch on his upstairs bedroom DVD player attached to his television. He could now watch an episode any time he wanted— and he did. As time went on, he began to complain to us that something was wrong with his bedroom television. Every time Rick or I would go to his room to see what was wrong, we'd find that he had several DVDs jammed into his DVD player. Being an electrical engineer, Rick would dismantle the DVD player and repair whatever was damaged as a result. John would insert a DVD, watch and enjoy the program, then simply turn it off, forgetting to remove the DVD. When he went to watch another episode, he'd try to insert the disc, not remembering that the last watched DVD was still in the player. Either Rick or I would try and train him to remove a DVD after he watched it, but John wasn't able to grasp the concept of removing it. Perhaps he was conditioned to think that it was just another television show on some channel, so there was no need to remove anything? No one will know. As time went on, he even had trouble remembering how to insert a DVD.

John slowly began to show signs of instability when he walked. His feet bothered him for years, so at first we thought that his careful gait was due to that. He began to take a cane with him on his walks round the block, which was a good thing. One evening as he was walking in their kitchen wearing only socks on his feet, John slipped on the floor and fell, banging his head on the grab handle of the oven door. Mary was upstairs but heard the loud thud below. As she quickly hobbled down the stairs, sliding down on her behind, she soon found John on the kitchen floor trying to get up. He couldn't, so Mary called Rick to come over and help, as he lived around the corner. The wide grab handle on the oven door of their kitchen stove was noticeably dented inward where he had hit it with his head as he went down. John told us that someone made a loud, whirring noise that frightened him and caused him to fall. He said, "The devil made me do it."

The Home Depot ® store was close to their home, so Mary relied on its proximity to make short trips to pick up items that were necessary for home maintenance and simple repair. She would always take John, both to give him a change of scenery and also because she was afraid to leave him home alone for any length of time. As she went up and down the aisles looking for an item she needed, John would often wander off if she wasn't watching him all the time. If she couldn't find him she would go to the customer service desk and describe him to the staff. They would then alert all the floor clerks to be on the lookout for this "missing person." The staff at Home Depot were wonderful. They would always find John in some part of the store where you would least expect him to be and bring him to Mary.

———∞———

"I see nothing, I know nothing!"

- Sergeant Schultz, Hogan's Heroes
(John would always laugh as
he imitated Sergeant Schultz.)

———∞———

Demolition Derby Day

It was Sunday, August 21st, 2011—a warm, sunny, lazy late summer day in the Southern Tier of New York. John had driven to his favorite watering hole, Dunkin' Donuts® on Main Street in Binghamton. He started going to Dunkin' Donuts some years earlier when he worked as a janitor at his nearby church. He took the part time janitor job after he retired from Ozalid Corporation as a paper machine operator. John always made friends easy, so between his long time buddies and newer friends he had met at Dunkin' Donuts, they all got together three or four times a week to *"smoke and joke"* (Army slang for have coffee, a doughnut, and plenty of good conversation). John was due home soon as Mary had told him they were going to make barbequed chicken on the backyard grill later that afternoon.

A neighbor woman who lived across the street from John and Mary told us that she saw John driving down their street at a higher than normal speed. She immediately saw that he was driving too fast, but before she could yell out to him, John made a sharp left turn into his driveway. The garage door was open but the section of the garage to the left of the open door is what stopped him. His driver's side front fender took out the wood and aluminum trim to that left side as he plowed into it and came to a stop. Mary was sitting on their nearby back porch. She screamed as she heard the loud crashing of the car against the garage frame, now ripped to pieces. She called Pat and I, and Rick and Kathy immediately.

52

Kathy and Rick could walk over as they were around the corner, but we were all there within minutes.

It was a sight to behold. John's car sat in front of the garage, splintered wood and bent aluminum siding scattered over the car and driveway. John was walking around his backyard swinging both arms in a huge windmill-like circular motion, just as he had done in California in 1984 when he almost took the two of us to our greater reward by falling asleep at the wheel. His motions were exactly as they were then. I was having a déjà vu moment.

The garage, Sunday, August 21, 2011

Two weeks and $1,500 later, a local contractor had temporarily removed the garage door so he could repair and rebuild the garage framework that had been destroyed. He finished by replacing the white aluminum siding on the exterior wall, and it was as good as new.

That demolition derby ended John's driving career forever. He kept trying to find and take the car keys that Mary hid in different places in their house. We finally were able to have his physician convince him that the police have his license number and will arrest him if he's caught driving! For months after that we'd find John in the garage, sitting in the car for hours, playing with all the control knobs.

———∝∞———

"I had been driving for forty years when I fell asleep at the wheel and had an accident."

———∝∞———

A New Taxi Service Begins

In spite of John demolishing the front of their garage that Sunday afternoon in August of 2011, the Dunkin' Donuts trips continued, except now by taxi: Mary's taxi, Pat's taxi, Rick's taxi, Kathy's taxi, and

Nick's taxi. He enjoyed these visits with his friends so much that one of us would pick him up, drop him off, and return an hour or two later to bring him back home.

On one of his early "taxi" trips, Pat took him but I had to bring him home, so I finished mowing my lawn, then I drove to Dunkin' Donuts to get him. I walked in and saw John sitting at a table near the front window with his friends. The four men and two ladies were chatting away as I approached their table. I was wearing a black baseball cap with the white letters "DW" on the front of the cap, which stands for "Drum World," a place where I often bought my musical supplies. As I walked up to John, he looked at me, gave me a wrinkled, sly smile, and said, "DW? Dim Wit! I'd like you all to meet my son-in-law!"

His friends immediately began ribbing me over that one! We all had a good laugh, but most important to me, John was smiling and happy at that moment.

John at Dunkin' Donuts, August 2014

Some months later, John's subtle changes in behavior were becoming more apparent to the family, and even to his friends at that point. I was driving him home from Dunkin' Donuts when he asked me, "When did you get her?"

I was confused, and replied, "Her? What her?" I was

alone in my car with him at that moment. He replied, "My wife." Apparently he saw Mary in my car—or thought he did?" A few minutes later during one of his now infrequent lucid moments, he told me that he knew that something was wrong with him. He didn't know what it was, and he was frightened because he didn't know what to do about it. We were stopped at a red light, so I looked into his eyes and said, "Don't worry, we're all here to take care of you." His eyes welled up with tears. They didn't flow, but the tears were there. I quickly put on one of his favorite CDs of Czech brass band music and he soon became lost in the world that he enjoyed so much.

On another of his Dunkin' Donuts trips, I took John there and we went to the counter to order his coffee and doughnut before he sat down with his friends, who were already at their usual table near the front window. The girls who worked the counter all knew John by name now. When one of them came over to us to take his order, John asked for coffee but didn't know what else to get with it. I asked him if he wanted a doughnut and he said "Yeah." I asked, "What kind?"

With a perplexed look on his face he muttered, "The kind I like!" I told the gal one Boston Creme doughnut, his favorite. As she brought the order she said, "$2.51 with your senior discount, John." He opened his wallet and gave her two $1 bills, and then a $5 bill. She looked at him with the most confused look as I told her, "Take it from the five dollar bill." She gave me his two one dollar bills back.

As time went on, Mary had cut back on her taxi service some because her painful right knee was becoming worse. I took them both to church one Sunday morning, then returned after the service to pick them up and drive them to a nearby community center to celebrate her friend, Mary's, 100th birthday. John came out of church a few minutes ahead of Mary, and as he sat down in the front seat of my car he asked, "Are you coming with us?" I told him no, I was just driving them to the community center and returning later to bring them home. He then said, "Is she coming?" Confused, I replied "Yes, of course," to which he responded, "Does she have to?" By that time Mary was getting into my car. As I drove away, John asked both of us, "Where are we going anyway?" Having had to deal with this endless repetition for months now, Mary was understandably frustrated as she said, "John, I told you ten times already today, we're going to Mary's 100th birthday party." John simply stared out the car window.

During these days of early dementia, Mary was already beginning to feel the stress of full time caregiving. Pat would often call her mother in the morning, and on one particular morning when she asked Mary where

Dad was, Mary replied, "I don't know, and you know what, I don't care." A few weeks after that, Mary decided she needed a break from it all, so she asked if we could watch John while she went out for an hour or so to relax. Mary became her own taxi service that day. We were going to be at home, so Pat agreed and Mary brought John over before she left. John and I watched a baseball game on television, then he went outdoors with me as I did some yard work. He wandered off while I was trimming some grass, but my neighbor stopped him as he was walking up the street toward the main road. He kept him talking while he called for me to tell me that he had John. An hour or so turned into well over four hours, and still no Mary. Pat finally called her mother on her cell phone and asked where she was. "Still at the casino," she replied. "Casino?" Pat exclaimed. Pat then told her that it was OK to have us watch John but if she had planned to be away all afternoon, she should have told us. Mary replied, "I can't take it anymore, I needed a break." She was already burning out, but doing the best she could under the circumstances.

Pat put on an extra piece of chicken on the grill and John stayed with us for dinner that afternoon.

———⫘———

"Caring for an individual with Alzheimer's

> *disease or a related dementia can be challenging and, at times, overwhelming. Frustration is a normal and valid emotional response to many of the difficulties of being a caregiver."*
>
> *- Family Caregiver Alliance; National Center on Caregiving; www.caregiver.org*

———◯∞◯———

T'was Three Weeks Before Christmas

It was 4:00 PM on Wednesday, the 4th of December 2013. It was a cloudy and cold twilight afternoon, but it wasn't snowing so the roads weren't slippery. The reason I mention the weather, time of day, and road conditions will soon become apparent. I had just arrived home from work and sat down to a nice dinner Pat had prepared, when the phone rang. It was Mary. She was in a panic. She told us that she thought John was upstairs in his room watching TV all afternoon. When she called him for dinner and he didn't answer she crawled upstairs, only to find the TV still playing, but no John. She then bundled up and went outdoors to look for him when her neighbor told her that she had seen John walking down the street several hours ago! I asked Mary if she could describe what she last remembered seeing John wearing. She said that she thought he had his heavy maroon jacket and blue and red ski cap on earlier in the day. So much for a nice, quiet dinner after a day's work.

I called my brother-in-law, Rick, to explain what had happened, and we decided to split up to see if either of us might stumble upon John somewhere nearby. Rick went to the mall just a block away from John's house and I headed for Dunkin' Donuts on Reynolds Road, just past the mall. The Dunkin' Donuts John always went to was on Main Street in Binghamton, but he liked them in general, so maybe he saw their sign and wandered toward it. I went inside and asked the manager if she had seen this man recently, showing her a picture of John. She had! She said he was there at least an hour earlier, then he left. "Just great," I thought. It was almost 5:00 PM on a weekday. It was rush hour traffic, three weeks before Christmas, traffic in and around the mall was bumper to bumper, and John might be somewhere in that mess trying to maneuver about on foot.

He would have had to cross two major, busy roads on foot to get to the only other nearby store, Wegmans Supermarket. (Pronounced with a hard "g" as in "great." John however, always pronounced it "Wedgemans.") At that point I figured it's the last local place to try, so I drove into Wegmans parking lot. It was packed with cars, so I slowly started driving up and down each parking aisle. All of a sudden, I spotted what looked like a blue and red ski cap near the entry/ exit doors. Could it be John? I parked my car illegally and quickly ran toward the man wearing the cap before he got away. As I got closer I saw the maroon jacket. It was John! He had stopped some complete stranger, a man leaving the store with his groceries, asking him how to get to the candy aisle. Thank God the man was a congenial fellow, as he told me that John had spent the last five minutes trying to convince him to take a trip together to the Czech Republic! He told him all about the wonderful music they would hear. I explained the problem to the man and thanked him for his understanding.

John smiled as I took him into the store, assuring him that I knew where the candy aisle was. As we were walking toward it, John said, "I like fireballs! I get my best shave with them!" I was so used to his conversations taking such drastic U-turns by now that I simply agreed and told him that fireballs candies do indeed give you a really close shave. As soon as we got to the self-serve candy bins, John began to fill up a large plastic bag with assorted candies, stopping every so often to unwrap and eat one. I told him that he shouldn't eat them before we pay for them, but he assured me that it was OK.

The large bag was finally filled with all his selected assortment of candies, so we headed down the main aisle toward the checkout registers. John was right be-hind me, as I made him hold on to me with one arm. As we kept walking I began to notice customers staring strangely in our direction. I turned around to see John taking his upper denture in and out of his mouth with his free hand. Being a dental hygienist, this didn't bother me in the least, but I can only imagine what kind of a nut job those customers thought I had tagging along with me! As we went to pay, John told me that he was rich as he grabbed for his wallet. His wallet was empty. I paid for the candy and wished John a Merry Christmas.

In my excitement and relief to have found John, I completely forgot to call Mary, Rick, or Pat! I called Rick, who was still at the mall, and told him to go home. As I drove John home and we walked into his house, Mary greeted us with both a sigh of relief and some angry words for John for wandering off without telling her. She was still struggling to understand this disease, and it was wearing her down; day by day, like Chinese water torture. She had called the police dur-ing the time I was searching, so she called them back to tell them that he had been found.

Two hours after it began, I again sat down to a nice, re-heated piece of steak and a baked sweet potato, along with a tossed salad.

—⟳⟲—

"But I heard him exclaim, ere he drove out of sight, Happy Christmas to all, and to all a good-night!"

- from the T'was The Night Before Christmas Poem, by Major Henry Livingston, Jr.

CHAPTER 5

Reaching Out For Help

Asking For Advice

MARY WAS UNDERSTANDABLY becoming more worried as the mishaps and unusual behavior of her husband were becoming more prevalent. As I alluded to earlier in the book, Mary is a proud woman who ran a wonderful household. She was firmly in control of the business of running a home and a family, but the day to day changes unfolding before her very eyes were slowly taking control of her physical and mental ability to cope.

In August of 2013 she asked me to take her to visit a local law firm that specialized in Senior law to gather information on what options were available to the family if John's condition worsened to the point where she could no longer handle him at home. At this point in time, Mary still used the word *"if"* in spite of the undeniable evidence that dementia and Alzheimer's disease are irreversible and have no cure. She wished for a miracle (who wouldn't), but had finally taken the first steps to face the inevitable.

The Friday, August 2nd, 2013 meeting with a Senior law attorney gave Mary and I useful information. We learned that if John needed to go to a nursing home at the highest level of care (skilled nursing), he could apply for Medicaid immediately, since their assets would dwindle quickly in a skilled nursing setting. Second, John needed a thorough evaluation by a nurse and a social worker. The county CASA Agency (Community Alternative Systems Agency) needed to evaluate John. CASA performs a comprehensive assessment, care planning, and level of care determination for county residents of any age or income level. Another invaluable evaluation should also be performed by someone who specializes in elder care matters. Third, since John was a United States veteran, we should contact the local Veteran's Administration (VA) office to begin the process of applying for a VA pension for John, something Mary had never even thought about before.

He gave us a brief, but useful explanation of the levels of care that may be offered at different nursing homes, listed here in order of least to most care required.

Independent Living

Independent living is usually the term used when someone is still independent, but lives in a room or an apartment located at a nursing home facility.

ACF (Adult Care Facility)

Adult Care Facilities serve persons requiring 24 hour supervision who are unable to live alone, by providing room, board, housekeeping, minimal personal care, assistance with basic activities of living, and supervision of their medications.

Assisted Living

Assisted living care is an intermediate level of long-term care with varying levels of supervision and personal or medical care. It offers a greater degree of care than ACF, but the residents are medically stable.

Skilled Nursing Care

Skilled Nursing Care centers, or nursing homes, offer 24-hour staffing to provide comprehensive services to those requiring a greater level of care than that offered by assisted living facilities. All Skilled Nursing Care centers require 24-hour medical care, utilizing the professional skills of a registered nurse (RN) or a licensed practical nurse (LPN).

As expected, the cost for the increased levels of professional care increase accordingly.

———∞———

"You gain strength, courage, and confidence by every experience in which you really stop to look fear in the face. You must do the things which you think you cannot do."

— Former First Lady Eleanor Roosevelt

———∞———

Marge

I've had the pleasure of caring for many very special patients in my second career as a registered dental hygienist, but one in particular stands out. She's a certified geriatric care manager who owns her own practice called Elder Care Management Solutions. I knew of her skills from our conversations in the dental office, so in January of 2014 I called Marjorie (Marge) Tubbert to give her an overview of our family situation that had been unfolding for some time now. We had several more discussions between January and March before we arranged for Marge to visit John and Mary to conduct an initial assessment of their situation. That assessment took place on Wednesday, April 2nd, 2014. The primary goal of this assessment was to objectively evaluate John and Mary's status, and determine the options that would best serve their current and future needs. Pat, Rick, Kathy, and I were unanimous in our support to keep John and Mary as independent as possible, but we had genuine concerns for their safety as their health and self-care needs increased. Among other things, Marge wanted to address home safety and also look into providing some respite care for Mary, as Marge already knew from our conversations that she was feeling the increased stress associated with being John's 24/7 caregiver.

As Marge became acquainted with them both, John instinctively turned on his easygoing nature, complete with a sly smile and wisecracks. After about five minutes into their getting to know one another, Marge became so taken by John that she blurted out, "Oh my, I could just take him home!" Marge could see that John's confusion was evident, however, and also that Mary's stamina as a caregiver was compromised by her chronic back, leg, and knee pain.

Marge performed a mental status screen with John, called the Mini-Mental State Exam and Clock Test. Its purpose was to screen for cognitive and/or memory impairment. John's scores were low, as expected. They indicated moderate cognitive functioning and diminished executive functioning, which relates to his ability to make sound and safe judgments. One of the questions that Marge asked John was when his birthday was. John immediately replied, "June 22nd," which was correct. She then asked him, "What year?" John quickly replied, "Every year!" After we all shared a good laugh over his answer, Marge said, "He's right," even though she was looking for the year of his birth.

Marge could see that John couldn't perform some of the basic activities of daily living, such as personal money management, laundering, cooking, or shopping. He exhibited weak muscle strength and was at risk for falls.

Marge and I then went through the entire house, room by room, while she asked me how they used different rooms and the items in them. She took many notes and later made suggestions on how to improve the safety of their in-home living. A little over one week after that initial assessment, she sent us all a 10-page Assessment Summary and Care Recommendation Report that included suggestions for bringing in a caregiver for a few hours several times a week to allow Mary some respite care, while engaging John in some stimulating activities and some light exercise. The one sentence in that report that stood out for me said, *"Ideally, assistance should be implemented before their needs increase, instead of delaying until caregiver burnout or a crisis occurs."*

In the weeks following the initial assessment, Marge

and I talked often. She coached me through various possible scenarios, such as potential nursing home placement for John, or how to go about looking for the best methods to handle their assets, which were not substantial. They included ownership of their home and a modest amount of money in savings accounts and IRAs, all of which would rapidly disappear if a nursing home for John became a reality.

One of Marge's biggest concerns was Mary's ability to safely care for John at home. At the initial assessment, she could see how Mary would threaten John with nursing home placement if he didn't "do better and pay more attention to things." Mary was already extremely frustrated with the situation because such threats are a hallmark sign of a burned out caregiver doing the best she can under difficult circumstances.

A month later (May 28th 2014), Marge and I continued with what I now called our "fireside chats." Once again, Marge strongly suggested that John needed structure and routine, not boredom. One way to achieve that was to take John to our local Adult Social Day Care Program at the local senior center. Marge even volunteered to initially take him there herself so she could observe how he would adapt to it. Unfortunately, Mary was not in favor of it, as she told us that she "knew" that John wouldn't like it. I know that one of Mary's chief concerns was money, even though the cost for these visits to the Day Care Program was quite minimal. In her mind, Mary could see that John was destined for a nursing home, so she was extremely worried that the enormous monthly cost for that would put a large dent in her ability to continue to afford to live at home. Mary was always figuring out costs and trying to come up with ways to make everything continue to work financially for them both.

In her May 28th 2014 email to me, Marge asked how their home situation was at present, and how they were both doing. I had just talked with Mary and also her neighbor the day before, so I shared the latest news of the day with her. What follows is an excerpt from my email to Marge that day:

"As for things around the house, John seems to be slowly getting a bit worse. He's beginning to lose track of day vs. night. He gets up at 10:00 PM and starts making his breakfast. He places the weekly trash out to the curb on days that it's not scheduled for pickup. Mary has him put it back alongside the garage, but he often simply takes it to the curb again. Mary now has to help him shower, because otherwise he will not initiate one, and when he does go in the shower, he doesn't do anything. If he's left alone to shower, his washcloth and towels are dry. She has to cue him and help wash him. When I talked with her neighbor

yesterday, he told me that he went over to see Mary in her back yard because he saw her sitting there, crying. Mary told him that she doesn't know what to do anymore. Plus, she continues to hobble around on a painful, bum right knee--yikes! Aren't you sorry you asked?"

Marge was everything I expected she would be, and then some. Her experience in the geriatric field was obvious. Her caring, sincerity, and patience were always present in all she did. Over the next year and beyond, Marge and I continued to talk via telephone calls and emails when I felt that an issue needed her expertise and insight. She is a superb resource and a truly wonderful lady, and her wisdom leaves me forever indebted to her.

───⟨∞⟩───

"It does not matter how long you are spending on the earth, how much money you have gathered or how much attention you have received. It is the amount of positive vibration you have radiated in life that matters,"

- Amit Ray, Meditation: Insights and Inspirations

(Marge has an abundance of positive vibration.)

The VA Is Contacted

At Mary's request, I called the Binghamton branch of the New York State Department of Veteran's Affairs Office on April 24th, 2014. The Senior law attorney we spoke to eight months prior suggested that we contact them then, but when Marge reinforced that suggestion at our initial assessment three weeks earlier, it finally reminded Mary that this matter needs attention—now! No more waiting and watching.

I talked with Mr. George S. Welles, Veterans counselor. He explained what we needed to do and we set up an initial meeting with him, Mary, and me on Monday, June 2nd, 2014. We went to his office at the Veteran's Affairs Department in downtown Binghamton, and George explained everything we needed to do to begin the process of applying for a Veteran's Administration (VA) pension for John. (Little did I realize that it would be almost one year later before John's VA pension would finally be approved.)

I would visit George at his office many times within the months that followed, as we worked through all the details required to obtain John's VA pension approval. I found him to be extremely helpful and dedicated to the care of all our veterans.

—∞—

"Life, Liberty and the Pursuit of All Who Threaten It"

- words and painting of a U.S. Naval Vessel hanging on the office wall of Mr. George S. Welles

CHAPTER **6**

A Brief Overview
of Dementia

Highlights

AT THIS POINT in our story, it's time to better acquaint you with the illness known as dementia. In simple terms, just what is dementia?

Dementia is a loss of cognitive functioning—thinking, remembering, and reasoning—along with a loss of behavioral abilities. It can eventually become severe enough to interfere with all aspects of a person's daily life. There are multiple causes for dementia, but Alzheimer's disease is the most common cause, accounting for about 60 to 80% of all dementia cases. In Alzheimer's Disease, the person's brain cells degenerate, shrink, and eventually die. This loss of brain cells over time is what brings on a steady decline in the person's memory, proper thinking skills, and normal behavior. In fact, the physical changes to brain cells related to Alzheimer's disease begin years before any signs of the disease.

Alzheimer's disease was named after Dr. Alois Alzheimer. In 1906, he examined the brain tissue of a woman who had passed away of an unusual mental illness, and found many abnormal clumps and tangled bundles of fibers. These clumps and tangled fibers are still some of the main features of Alzheimer's disease, along with the loss of connections between nerve cells (neurons) that transmit messages between different parts of the brain. They also transmit messages from the brain to muscles and organs of the body.

According to the Alzheimer's Association, the 2016 information shows that over five million Americans are living with Alzheimer's disease, and up to sixteen million will have the disease by the year 2050. Over a threefold increase in just over 30 years is clearly an epidemic increase. Alzheimer's disease is already the sixth leading cause of death in the United States. One in three seniors currently die from Alzheimer's disease or another form of dementia.

Alzheimer's disease worsens over time. It is an irreversible, progressive disease, and although the greatest known risk factor is increasing age, it is not just a disease of old age. Up to 5% of those affected by the disease have younger-onset Alzheimer's, which can affect someone as early as their 40s or 50s. There is presently no cure for Alzheimer's disease. In fact, Alzheimer's is the only disease in the top ten causes of death in America that cannot be prevented, cured, or even appreciably slowed.

Some world famous people have been unfortunate enough to suffer from Alzheimer's disease. In 1983, U.S. President Ronald Reagan designated November as National Alzheimer's Awareness Month. Six years after his presidency, he would fall victim to the disease himself. He announced his condition to all Americans in an effort to raise public awareness of the disease. Actor Charlton Heston also publicly announced that he suffered from Alzheimer's disease, as did other celebrities such as singer, Glen Campbell, and actress, Rita Hayworth.

Caregivers

Alzheimer's disease takes a devastating toll on caregivers, involving high physical, emotional, and financial costs. Nearly 60% of Alzheimer's and dementia caregivers rate the emotional stress of caregiving as high or very high, and 40% suffer from depression themselves. Seventy-five percent of caregivers report being somewhat to very concerned about their own health since becoming a caregiver. Many of them don't ask for help even though they desperately need it.

The caregiver issue is so important and challenging that when I mentioned my writing this book to a physician I know quite well, he readily shared his personal feelings on the subject with me, as he was a caregiver himself until his parent passed away. The following are his thoughts on the subject. They serve to underscore the statistics just presented:

As a caregiver, I eventually felt all of the negative aspects that are commonly associated with that role; feeling frustrated, overworked, and depressed by the reality of having to deal with a disease that has no positive outcome. You have to be able to tell yourself that it's OK for a caregiver to wish for the patient to die peacefully. It's not mean, and it doesn't mean that the caregiver no longer cares. They know all too well the void that will be left by that person's passing, but the burden of the caregiver eventually becomes so overwhelming that it can bring them to the point where they feel they can no longer handle it.

Some Typical Signs

What follows are some of the more typical signs of Alzheimer's disease:

Memory Loss (Difficulty Remembering Newly Learned Information.) This is the most common early symptom, because Alzheimer's usually begins in the part of the brain that affects learning. Besides memory loss, they can forget important dates or events, and they might repeatedly ask for the same information.

Planning or Problem Solving Issues. They may experience changes in their ability to follow a plan, or work with numbers. Concentration becomes more difficult, and simple tasks may take much longer to do.

Difficulty Completing Familiar Tasks. People with Alzheimer's often find it difficult to complete a routine task. They may have trouble driving to a familiar location. They may be unable to manage the numbers to complete things like a budget. They may have forgotten how to play a familiar game.

Confusion with Time or Place. They may forget dates, seasons, and the passage of time. They may forget where they are.

Problems with Both Spoken or Written Words. They may have trouble speaking or writing the correct word, or simply use a wrong word in place of the right word.

Misplacing Things. They may put things in unusual places. They may accuse others of stealing.

Decreased or Poor Judgment. They may not know how to make simple monetary change. They may pay less attention to grooming or self-cleanliness.

Changes in Mood or Personality. They can become easily confused, fearful, depressed, or anxious.

In Part 2 of our story, you will witness most all of the signs just outlined come to life.

References:

(1) www.alz.org Alzheimer's Association – contains information on Alzheimer's disease and dementia.

(2) www.nia.nih.gov National Institute on Aging – conducts and supports research on aging and the health and well-being of older people.

PART TWO

AFTER THE STORM

CHAPTER 7

D-Day and Its Immediate Aftermath

D-Day Minus One

D-DAY MINUS ONE. It was 5:00 AM on Thursday July 31st, 2014. Kathy and Rick received a telephone call from Mary's alarm service telling them that the alarm that she wore around her neck for emergency use had just been triggered. They both ran out their door and around the corner to John and Mary's house to check on what was happening. Kathy stayed downstairs and Rick went up to her bedroom. Rick found her on the bedroom floor, wrapped in her blankets, shivering. She could not get up. They both tried to convince her that she needed to go to a doctor to be evaluated but Mary was insistent upon not going to the emergency room.

D-Day

D-Day, a term used in military circles as the name for the day an operation or event will take place. For World War 2 it was Tuesday, June 6th, 1944. For John's family, it was Friday, August 1st, 2014.

That Friday began as a typical summer day, warm and sunny. After I had a nice breakfast of cooked oatmeal along with some sliced mangoes in plain yogurt, I went for my morning walk outdoors. Pat usually called her mother in the morning to check on them both, but her first call went unanswered. She waited about ten minutes and tried again. Still no answer, so I decided to drive down and check on them. They only lived about a mile from us. I knew that John would probably still be in bed as he was always a late riser, but I hoped that Mary would be up and about by that time. She had been complaining of not feeling well for the past week, often sleeping until 1:00 or 2:00 PM in the afternoon—very unlike her. When Pat stopped by just the day before, it was 1:00 PM and she found Mary still sleeping. John was sitting near her bed in a small rocking chair just looking at her. He really was unaware of what to do.

I parked my car in the driveway and let myself in the front door. It was silent—too silent. I looked to my right into their family/TV room, and there was Mary—lying on the floor. She looked at me with obvious pain

85

on her face as she barely mumbled out the words, "I can't get up."

Besides her obvious pain, she was very pale, had chills because she was shivering, and she had very rapid, shallow breathing. I took her pulse and it seemed OK, not overly rapid or slow, and no sign of arrhythmia. I called Pat at home and we immediately agreed that I should call 9-1-1, which I did. I then tried to see if Mary could use her arms to help herself get up, but she was unable to move to any significant degree. Since she was in pain, I let her continue to lie still on the floor for fear that something was broken and moving her would make it worse, so after getting her some water to drink because her lips seemed parched, I just sat alongside her. She was unable to drink much. She was acting very confused and unable to carry on any real conversation.

Pat had called Kathy and she arrived within minutes. Within a very short time the ambulance arrived, which stirred up the people in the neighborhood. My immediate concern at that point, with all of the noise and commotion now taking place in the family room, was not waking John up. I explained to the EMT crew what I saw when I arrived that morning, along with what I had observed since then. They gently, carefully picked Mary up and placed her on a gurney, and then wrapped her in a blanket. I opened the front door all the way so that they could wheel her out onto the sidewalk, street, and into the back of the ambulance for her trip to the emergency room at St. Bernadette Hospital. Kathy had called Rick and he left work immediately, arriving just as they brought Mary outside her house on the gurney. John had been hard of hearing for a few years, but didn't wear his hearing aids to bed, so he didn't wake up through all of this. It was the first and only time that I was glad that he was hard of hearing!

—⚬✕⚬—

"Ideally, assistance should be implemented before their needs increase, instead of delaying until caregiver burnout or a crisis occurs."

- Marge Tubbert, an excerpt from her April 11th 2014 report titled "Assessment Summary and Care Recommendations for John and Mary"

—⚬✕⚬—

Two Weeks at St. Bernadette Hospital

Mary was examined in the emergency room at St. Bernadette Hospital. A CT scan was performed, along with other tests and a great deal of blood work. She was diagnosed with septicemia, also known as bacteremia, or blood poisoning. Septicemia is a serious blood infection caused by her body's immune system reacting to an infection somewhere in her body. It can lead to death if not treated promptly. The CT scan showed multiple abscesses on her liver. A normal white blood cell count is usually between 4,500 and 10,000 cells/microliter. An increase in white blood cells is typical in an active infection. Mary's white blood cell count was 35,000. We already knew that she had stage two kidney failure, diagnosed earlier in the year. She was admitted to St. Bernadette Hospital later that afternoon.

Mary would spend the next two weeks in the hospital receiving IV antibiotics and other medications, along with more tests, CT scans, blood draws, and physical therapy. As she slowly improved over those two weeks, the decision was made to eventually discharge her to a local nursing home for rehabilitation, as her recent illness coupled with her already bad knee would require rehabilitation if she were ever able to return home. Mary was insistent on being sent to River's Edge Nursing Home near downtown Binghamton, only several miles away from St. Bernadette Hospital. Her stay at the hospital amounted to charges of almost $60,000, but her Medicare HMO Advantage health insurance plan covered all but the $360 deductible hospital admission co-pay.

The next day, Pat and I took John to visit her at the hospital. We stopped by their house at about 1:00 PM and made sure that he was clean shaven and nicely dressed before we left. When we arrived, Mary was in bed as she was not yet well enough to be up and about. We were sitting in her hospital room talking when John told us that he had to go to the bathroom. There was a visitor's bathroom just down the hallway across from Mary's door, so Pat helped guide her father to it. She was waiting for what seemed like a very long time before she knocked on the bathroom door to ask John if everything was alright. As John opened the door, Pat saw that his pants were down around his knees and he had made a bowel movement, but he was just sitting there. She helped him clean up and walked with him back to Mary's room, but as they were walking down the hallway, John continued to have a bowel movement. Pieces of feces were falling on the hallway floor as they rolled down through his inner pant legs. He was walking through piles of his own excrement as Pat summoned a nearby hospital cleaning lady to ask if she could get someone to help him. This lady was a saint, perhaps even St. Bernadette in disguise. I know that she went far above and beyond her job description when she took it upon herself to walk John into Mary's bathroom to help clean him up. Mary was horrified by what had happened, and from her hospital bed she began to rhythmically chant, "nur-sing home, nur-sing home." There was no doubt that she was living with caregiver burnout already and this incident just re-ignited her defense mechanism. You may recall that in earlier months, Mary would threaten John with going to a nursing home if he didn't "straighten out." She still believed that he had it within his power to fix what was wrong with him. Mary was so shaken by this incident that she insisted we take John home as soon as possible.

The cleaning lady helped John put on a hospital pajama bottom and some hospital gripper socks, placing his soiled clothes in a plastic bag along with his soiled shoes. She then brought a wheelchair for him so that Pat and I could wheel him to our car for the ride home. He was smiling and happy as we sat him down on the bed sheet covering the wheelchair, but I could hear the embarrassment in his voice as we left Mary. We maneuvered his wheelchair around all of the yellow signs that hospital maintenance people had placed atop the blotches of excrement on the floor. We placed John into the front seat of the car, using the bed sheet from the wheelchair for him to sit on. Hospital visitors walking by looked at us with puzzled expressions as we placed this smiling man into the car wearing hospital pajamas and gripper socks. Perhaps they thought we were helping this patient escape from the hospital? (My thoughts momentarily drifted back to hearing John tell us stories of his time spent working at this very hospital as a security guard. He used to help people just like the person he had now become.) The ride home was made as bearable as possible with the car windows rolled down. We threw his soiled underwear and pants in the trash, but I took his shoes and thoroughly, repeatedly scrubbed and hosed them down in their basement washtub and hung them out to dry on the clothesline in the late afternoon sun.

———◯✕◯———

"I am expecting Mary to resist all suggestions and struggle to keep the status quo until a crisis for one of them occurs. If she had an emergency, what would John do? The four of you would have to care for him without another plan in place. It's definitely time for some changes."

- Marge Tubbert, an excerpt from her email to me, April 17th, 2014

———◯✕◯———

John Leaves His Home Forever

John and Mary lived in their nice, well-kept Cape Cod home in Johnson City for sixty-six years. The

D-Day crisis opened new chapters in both their lives. On the afternoon of D-Day, August 1st, I called Marge to tell her that the crisis that we all feared had happened. She went right to work making calls to all the local nursing homes to see what availabilities there might be for John, and now, perhaps for Mary too. Mary's future was now very uncertain as a result of this life-threatening infection in her blood, so we had to anticipate worst case scenarios for them both. On this day, however, we needed to focus on finding a place for John as soon as possible. The clock was ticking.

We all did what was necessary to care for John until we could find him a new home that would meet his needs. I began calling nursing homes too, coordinating my efforts with Marge. Pat shopped for groceries to keep food in the house. She also tended to Mary at the hospital, keeping in close contact with the doctors and nursing staff and setting up appointments for Mary as she slowly progressed. By 2:00 PM on the afternoon of D-Day, August 1st, Kathy took John for a haircut, followed by a trip to nearby Dunkin' Donuts for coffee and a visit with his friends.

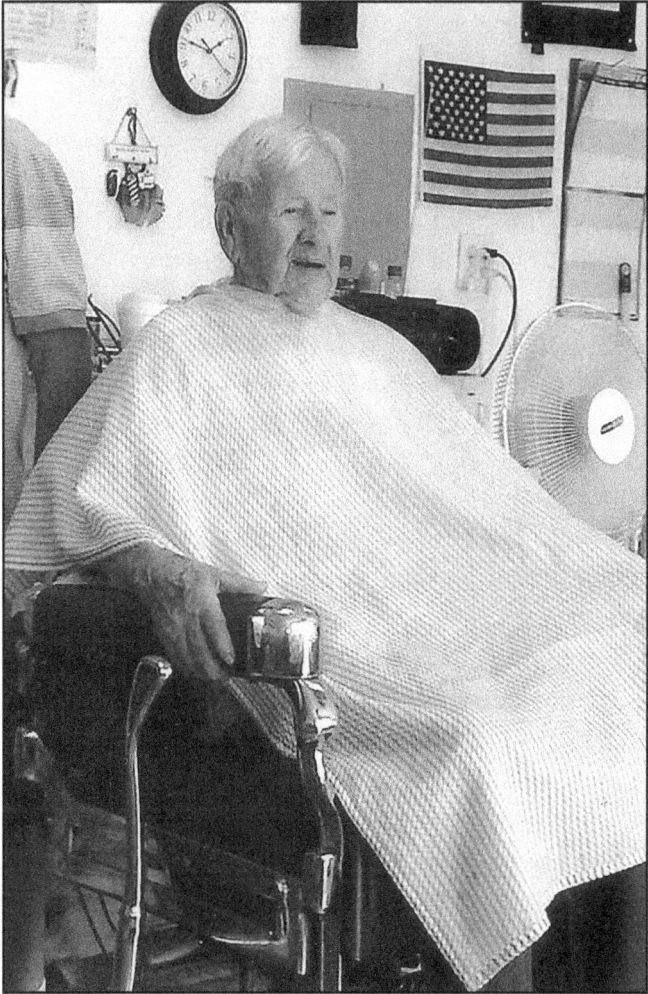

John at the barbershop, August 1, 2014

Kathy came over every day at mealtimes to make sure that John was eating properly and on time. She would make meals at home and bring them over for John to eat. She also took over caring for John's hearing aids and the batteries needed for them. Rick took on the job of sleeping at their house with John to make sure that John wasn't left alone at night. After three or four days, John had the new sleeping arrangement figured out, as he would turn the back porch light on for Rick before he came to spend the night. From her years working at Northpark Ridge, Pat knew that they had short term respite care available, so I called them before D-Day was over. I spoke with admissions coordinator Anne Gruber about our crisis. She explained to me that because John and Mary's assets were below what they require in order to offer permanent residency, they could not accept him for anything but a short, thirty day respite care stay, payable in advance. She had to meet John in person before his respite stay could occur, so we arranged a meeting for Wednesday, August 6th at 1:00 PM. As Marge put it, "Thirty days is thirty days; hopefully time enough to work out a permanent solution for John." Because Mary's prognosis was so uncertain at this time, no one really had a good idea whether either she or John could ever return home to live. This made the thirty day respite care stay make even more sense. It bought us precious time to plan and work matters out.

On Wednesday afternoon, August 6th, Pat and I picked up John at home and drove to Northpark Ridge to meet with Anne Gruber. We went over John's financial status as Anne talked with John, evaluating him. She took an immediate liking to John, as he was his typical humorous self with her, cracking jokes and little quips. He said to Anne, "Gruber. Sounds German? Are you a German?"

She chuckled as she told him that she wasn't German, it was her married name. John continued on with his comical questions and answers, and had Anne laughing throughout the entire interview. At the conclusion of our meeting, I had visited the finance office, filled out the necessary paperwork, and wrote a check for $7,988.64, post-dated for Friday, August 8th, his scheduled admission day. He would be living in a semi-private room at Northpark Ridge, starting on August 8th at 2:00 PM, and concluding on August 30th at 10:00 AM.

On Friday the 8th, myself, Pat, Kathy, and Rick packed John's suitcase with the clothes we felt he needed, along with the necessary toiletries. He was understandably confused, but we kept explaining to him that he was going for a small vacation until Mary was well enough to return home from the hospital. In reality, August 8th 2014 was John's last day in his home—forever. At about 1:00 PM, Kathy and Rick drove him to Northpark Ridge to begin his "vacation."

On Monday, August 11th 2014 we had a mid-morning doctor's appointment for John. Pat and I took him to see his doctor, Martin J. Smiško, MD, for an exam that was required for admission to Northpark Ridge, even though he began his stay there the prior Friday.

Mary was still in the hospital and not doing well. Her septicemia was improving but her liver abscesses were still a big concern. When Dr. Smiško came into the exam room, his immediate concern was the hospital report that he was reading concerning Mary, as he was her doctor too. He looked quite concerned as he completed reading it over in silence, then he looked at us and said, "I'm really sorry." Pat and I knew he was quite worried, but John just smiled and said, "Thanks, Doc." John's dementia was taking center stage again.

As he read Mary's medical notes, my thoughts drifted back to December of 1991. I remembered Dr. Smiško sitting and looking just as he did then, only in 1991 he was sitting at the nurses' station at St. Bernadette Hospital. Pat was a nurse consultant for adult care at Northpark Ridge in 1991 and assisted Dr. Smiško, who was medical director at Northpark Ridge in addition to having his own private practice. She asked him if he would take on my father as a patient, and he agreed. My father was in St. Bernadette Hospital suffering from what we didn't know was cancer of the liver yet, and we wanted a second opinion and a change of physicians, as my father's doctor was "less than thorough." Dr. Smiško read my father's records and test results, then came into his hospital room, sat on the edge of his bed and spoke these words to him. "You have cancer of the liver and it will take your life." My father smiled a slight smile, looked at my mother and said, "Bye."

Dr. Smiško was a brilliant diagnostician, so when he was worried, we all had good reason to worry about Mary.

John adapted quite well to Northpark. He had always been quick to strike up a conversation with anyone, and in 2014 he was still lucid enough to be able to do that. The staff all took an immediate liking to him, including the cleaning people. He was a friendly, easygoing guy. The dining room on John's floor had an open concept with a lounge area immediately adjacent to the dining area. One day during his first week, John was engrossed in a movie on the television in the lounge titled "The Glenn Miller Story" starring Jimmy Stewart. An aide came to move him to the dining area for lunch, but he wouldn't go. He had to watch the movie! Perhaps his mind was going back to 1944 when John saw the real Glenn Miller, Captain Glenn Miller and his American Band of the Army Air Force, perform in person inside the B24 airplane hangars at his air base in England. The nursing staff made up a tray for him so that he could have his lunch in the lounge while watching the movie. He was happy, and thanked them for bringing his lunch so he could watch the movie.

During the month of August, Marge had been working her contacts at four area nursing homes and two family-type homes for adults, in an effort to place John in one of them. I had filled out nursing home applications for both John and Mary and submitted them to those homes that were possibilities for one or both of them (still not knowing what the outcome was to be for Mary). Marge already knew of John's growing problem with incontinence, and felt that issue would likely be the barrier that could keep John from being admitted into an assisted living environment. We filled out applications for both John and Mary to the parent organization, Unified Christian Communities, and I hand-delivered them on Friday, August 8th. During that afternoon, Kathy and Rick took John to Northpark Ridge to begin his respite stay. The three separate homes; Islington House, Westmoor Hall, and Sunrise Knoll were all run by the parent company, Unified Christian Communities. Marge felt that John might do well at the assisted living unit for dementia at the Sunrise Knoll campus, but she wanted us to report to her on how often John needed assistance using the bathroom after he had been at Northpark Ridge for a week. In particular, she wanted to know if he had been incontinent in bed or in his clothing. Fortunately he seemed to manage better than we expected during his stay at Northpark Ridge, so Marge was able to work her magic and secure a permanent move to the Sunrise Knoll Assisted Living Dementia Unit for John! It was tentatively scheduled to move John from Northpark Ridge to Sunrise Knoll on Tuesday, August 26th 2014; five days before his stay at Northpark Ridge was scheduled to end.

On his last day at Northpark Ridge, Pat and I arrived to pack and get John ready to move. Kathy and Rick packed his belongings while Pat and I took care of financial and nursing matters related to the transfer. The staff were all teary-eyed to see John go. In less than three weeks, John had wormed his way into their hearts. As we were walking down the hallway toward the elevator, a cleaning lady came running down the hall pushing her mop and rolling bucket. She just had to say goodbye. She was crying as she hugged John and wished him well. It was a warm and sunny day outdoors, but inside Northpark Ridge at that moment, it was raining.

—∞—

> *"Remember me and smile, for it's better to forget than to remember me and cry."*
>
> *- Dr. Seuss*

———⚬⚬⚬———

Rehab at River's Edge

Mary made such a fuss about returning home to live during her two weeks at St. Bernadette that Rick and I took the time to convert the first floor TV room at their house into her new, first floor bedroom. We brought her bed, dresser, and night stand from her upstairs bedroom, and arranged the furniture so she had easy access to everything. But it was not to be. The reality of the situation was that Mary wasn't well or stable enough to be left alone at home. At a minimum, she needed some short-term rehabilitation.

On Friday, August 15th, two weeks after she had been admitted to the hospital, Mary was transported by medi-van from St. Bernadette Hospital to River's Edge nursing home for rehabilitation. Mary had been very ill, so she spent much of the time in bed while in the hospital. Her bad right knee hadn't had nearly enough use to keep her walking without stumbling and severe pain. She was assigned a semi-private room. During her stay at River's Edge, she often had cranky roommates, which didn't help matters. Initially, she occupied the bed away from the window, so she had no outside view at all. Eventually she was given the window bed, so her view was that of the rear parking lot along with the hills of Binghamton in the distance. Her window bed faced north, so there was no direct sunlight shining into her room.

She constantly complained about the terrible food. She would often ask us to stop by the local Taco Bell ® restaurant on the way over, and bring her a soft flour taco to replace whatever was on her menu that day. Needless to say, with all that had happened to her and John during the last two weeks, she was very depressed.

Less than a week after her arrival at River's Edge, Mary was getting worse, not better. Pat was talking to her on the phone the evening of Thursday, August 21st, when Mary said that she had to try and get out of bed and start her day. Pat was stunned. "Day? It's night time! Look out your window," Pat replied.

"No it's not, it's daytime," Mary said. Pat went to River's Edge early the next morning to find her mother unresponsive, so she called Connie Juliet to Mary's room. Connie was the nurse practitioner covering the floor that day, and also a friend of Pat's from the days when Pat was the supervising evening nurse at Northpark

Ridge some ten years earlier. Connie examined Mary and told the charge nurse that she needed to go to the emergency room immediately. At 10:00 AM on Friday, August 22nd, Mary was transported by medi-van to St. Bernadette's ER once again, exactly three weeks after her first visit. Pat called Rick, Kathy, and I as she drove to St. Bernadette behind the medi-van. We all arrived as quickly as possible.

When I saw Mary in the ER, she was essentially unresponsive. She barely opened her eyes at all, and barely slurred out Pat and Rick's names at one point. Kathy, Rick, and I talked in the hallway while Pat sat in the room with Mary. I told them that Marge had just informed me less than an hour ago that John had been accepted at Sunrise Knoll and would be moving there on Monday! We were elated at that wonderful news; while at the same time, we looked into Mary's room and saw the gaunt face of a woman at death's door. It gave us all new meaning to the phrase "mixed emotions."

Since Mary had a Do Not Resuscitate (DNR) Order stating that her wishes were that she be kept comfortable, the ER doctors and nurses made the decision to just transport her back to River's Edge, which happened by mid-afternoon that day. Kathy and I began planning Mary's potential funeral. We both spent most all of Saturday digging through pictures of her and selecting the ones we felt would be good to display at the funeral home. We pooled our efforts online by sharing our pictures, and by day's end we had them chosen.

It was quite obvious to Kathy, Rick, Pat, and myself that we should sell their small car, a Ford Focus. John hadn't driven in almost three years, and with Mary virtually at death's door, we could use the money from the sale of the car for their care. Kathy and Rick knew a good, honest guy who dealt with used cars. He gave us a fair price so they took the car to him, then I went to the Department of Motor Vehicles to turn in the license plates. I called the auto insurance company to cancel their policy. The car was now just another memory.

Pat and I were convinced that Mary had suffered a TIA (Transient Ischemic Attack)—a mini-stroke, or a warning stroke. She was virtually in a coma Friday and Saturday. Pat went to church on Sunday morning, August 24th, while I stayed home to finish working on a layout for the selected pictures for the funeral home. It was 8:00 AM. The phone rang—the caller ID showed that it was River's Edge. My body froze with terror. I sat down and braced myself for the news I was about to be given. The charge nurse on Mary's floor then spoke these words to me, "I just wanted to let you know that Mary woke up just now and she wants something to eat!"

I was dumbfounded and immediately called Pat on her cell phone at church. Pat was just as stunned as

I had been when she saw that I was calling her in the middle of mass at church. She went outside and I relayed the news to her. She left church immediately and drove to River's Edge.

Mary has told us what I'm about to share with you many times since that day. In her words, "I was in my coma and heard a woman's voice tell me, "You've been sleeping long enough, get up!" I sat up, rang for the nurse, and asked for something to eat because I was hungry. No one ever believes me, but that's what happened."

Mary is convinced that it was her guardian angel. She remembers virtually nothing of those three days.

—∞—

"It's hard to let go. Even when what you're holding onto is full of thorns, it's hard to let go. Maybe especially then."

- Stephen King, author; from his novel, Joyland

—∞—

John's Escapades at Sunrise Knoll

I call John's life at Sunrise Knoll an escapade. There is no doubt his days spent there were an adventure, both in adapting to Sunrise Knoll and also in dealing with the problems and mishaps that happened along the way.

As the mid-day sun shone brightly on that warm August 26th day, Pat and I walked John out to our car in the Northpark Ridge parking lot. John was still able to walk without any help, but a bit slower than his usual, former pace. We took him the long way; through downtown Binghamton and across the Susquehanna River so that he could enjoy the ride and scenery along the way to his next home. He did enjoy it, making comments about the many beautiful trees standing tall on and around the islands in the Susquehanna. It was the last real automobile ride John ever took.

When we arrived at Sunrise Knoll, the receptionist at the front desk called the dementia unit on the 2nd floor and a nurse soon arrived to escort us to John's new room. Pat and I made a trip to the car to bring in his clothes and suitcase. Rick brought his television later that day and connected it. John had a nice private room with a window view overlooking the entrance drive to the campus. In the autumn days ahead, he would sit in his small rocking chair, brought from his lifelong home, and stare out that window for hours just watching the people coming and going. His wing of the dementia unit had their own small, intimate dining area at the south end of the wing, with a few tables to accommodate the residents assigned to it.

John told me many times that he really liked it. He would often go to the dining area during the day and just sit there and look out the windows at the trees and hills surrounding the campus. He had a good appetite, enjoying steak and all of the other wonderful meals served to the residents. Loretta, who was a long-time friend of the family, was admitted to the same floor within days of John. I remember seeing her the day she arrived. She looked at me, trying to figure out who I was, but she could no longer remember my name, or how we worked together over the years as officers in the local Czechoslovak Club. Her room was only two doors down from John. She and John would serenade their fellow dining room residents often by singing Slovak music as best they could at meal times.

As the days went by, John was using a cane more often as he was becoming less sure-footed. He was also becoming more confused as to his toileting schedule. His dementia unit was secured, but it was the only assisted living dementia unit in the area. All the others were classified as skilled nursing. This meant that he received some, but not rigorous nursing care throughout the day. John began to wake up and wander more during the night. The first incident occurred during one of those nighttime strolls. He was walking down the hallway toward the dining room area, wearing only a t-shirt, when he stopped alongside a yellow pedestal sign used by maintenance people to warn passers-by.

In this case it was placed to tell others that the floor was wet, as they had recently mopped it. John saw that sign with the words in Spanish and English—Piso Mojado, meaning wet floor. Afterwards John told me that the sign meant "piss here"—so he did. He urinated on the floor in the hallway next to the sign that he claimed told him this was the place to do that. A nurse saw him "watering the flowers" as she so nicely worded it, but from that point on they paid much more attention to his wandering and choice of "bathrooms."

John's new men's room sign, October 2014

His growing problem with instability became more of an issue too. On Saturday, October 18th, some seven weeks after he had arrived, a nurse found him on the floor in the hallway in the middle of the night. He sustained a closed head injury and was taken by ambulance to St. Bernadette's emergency room, where he had a CT scan of the head performed. We received the telephone call from the nurse on his floor shortly after it happened. We called Kathy and Rick, then we went to the emergency room where we met them. We found John on a stretcher in the hallway in the emergency room, joking with the people tending to him. Thankfully, nothing appeared broken and he was discharged back to Sunrise Knoll.

On Thursday, November 6th, he fell in his room. Once again he was sent to St. Bernadette's emergency room, evaluated for pulmonary function, and sent back to Sunrise Knoll. On Wednesday, November 12th, less than one week later, he fell in the hallway again. The emergency room kept him overnight for observation, taking care of several cuts and bruises that he had sustained. John continued on with his comical ways in spite of what had happened. I remember one male MD student caring for John laughing so hard he was doubled over! We weren't laughing, however, when it was soon discovered that both of his hearing aids had been lost during that emergency room visit. As Marge told me, "glasses, hearing aids, and dentures are the three most often lost items in nursing homes." This happened during a hospital stay, not a nursing home, but it really didn't matter where it happened. Bottom line, he no longer had a $3,000 set of hearing aids.

After repeated issues with urinating at will, coupled with multiple falls requiring trips to the emergency room, the decision was made to move John to a higher level of care: the secured, skilled nursing dementia unit at Islington House in Binghamton. It was a part of the same parent organization as Sunrise Knoll; Unified Christian Communities. That transfer took place on Wednesday, November 19th, 2014.

———∞———

"We can complain because rose bushes have thorns, or rejoice because thorn bushes have roses."

- U.S. President Abraham Lincoln

CHAPTER **8**

Reaching Out
for Help Continues

Enter An Elder Care Law Attorney

WITH THE MYRIAD of events that occurred in August of 2014, it looked as if John was headed for a nursing home and Mary seemingly destined for the same. I contacted Ms. Priscilla Mason, a prominent elder care law attorney in the area, to discuss a number of legal and administrative issues now coming to the forefront regarding their finances. Pat and I had our first meeting with Priscilla on Monday, August 25th, 2014, the day before John moved from respite care at Northpark Ridge to the Sunrise Knoll dementia unit.

Since John and Mary had limited savings that would dwindle rapidly if one or both of them should reside in a nursing home, the rules of Medicaid were explained in detail. The real issue facing the family on August 25th however was the state of flux that both John and Mary were in at that point. John was headed for an assisted living (not skilled nursing) dementia unit at a nursing home (Sunrise Knoll), and Mary's situation was still quite uncertain since she'd had a probable mini-stroke just three days prior. The likely prognosis at the time prompted Priscilla to recommend that we apply for Medicaid for Mary very soon, as she appeared to be headed for skilled nursing. Priscilla could take care of all the application work for us, but it would take a hefty sum of money out of their limited savings (easily thousands of dollars to do all the necessary applications). Their house would not be considered for Medicaid, but they would put a lien on it. On August 29th, I began the Medicaid application for Mary, at the same time making changes in their assets to benefit John, as he would now be living as a community spouse in the assisted living section of a nursing home. I began the process of transferring the joint ownership of their home to be in John's name only. That deed transfer was made official on October 3rd, 2014. Marge and I continued to exchange phone calls and emails, and it was her expert advice that helped us to keep this now listing ship reasonably upright in the months ahead.

Mary's dissatisfaction at River's Edge made her begin

to ask for a return to live at home once again. She said this knowing that she would be living there alone. In her present delicate mental and physical condition, this would not have been a wise move, and we continued to try and convince her of that reality.

The following are excerpts of an August 2014 email from Marge to me, presenting a realistic scenario of John and Mary's situation as of mid-August 2014:

> *"From a financial reality standpoint, particularly if Mary does well (a big "if" right now), the most prudent way to proceed would be:*
>
> - *Apply for Medicaid for her immediately to pay for her care and preserve their income/assets for John's care.*
>
> - *With John at Sunrise Knoll and the Medicaid application filed for Mary, they would not be pressured to hurry and sell their house because it will be his once you change the deed over to him. You would want a plan in place to get it sold so cash could be used to pay for his care as his other sources of money get low.*
>
> - *If River's Edge decides that she must be discharged, I would not encourage it before a safe plan is in place. They cannot discharge her to an unsafe plan.*

I'm sorry not to see/have an option that pleases Mary right now. Private care at home averages about $15 an hour. Imagine how many hours/ days per week of home care she would need if she actually returned home to live alone. Do the math. What would you do if Mary did go home to live, decided she likes it, accepted the expensive home care costs (a big "if'"), her assets continue to go down, and she suddenly required yet another hospitalization? This entire dreadful scenario will begin again, complete with another hunt for a quick nursing home rehab bed. Think it over. It's too late in their time of need. A plan that makes more sense, yet would still be acceptable to her is needed. There simply are not a lot of options, and somehow Mary needs to understand that reality." Marge

———⧗———

"We can't help everyone, but everyone can help someone"

- U.S. President Ronald Reagan

———⧗———

The VA Saga Continues

During the last quarter of 2014, my contacts with the VA and also veteran's counselor Mr. George S. Welles continued, as no reasonable progress had been made regarding John's April 2014 application for a VA pension. As Power of Attorney (POA) for John, I was allowed to represent him insofar as correspondence between the VA and John, since he had dementia. I received letters for John on August 14th, September 15th, and November 13th, 2014 from the Department of Veteran's Affairs in St. Paul, Minnesota, telling him that a backlog of work was resulting in a delay in processing his application. On November 25th, their next letter informed him that his application was denied because of excess funds.

I met with Mr. George S. Welles soon after, and we drafted a reply dated December 15th stating that they failed to use all of the information that had been given to them on VA Form VAF 21-0779, showing them the monthly expense of John's nursing home care. Mr. Welles requested a re-consideration of John's case based upon the additional expense of the nursing home private pay rate of $187 per day. I received another letter from the Department of Veteran's Affairs in Philadelphia, Pennsylvania dated January 6th, 2015, telling me what the prior August, September, and November letters did; they were backlogged and the decision on his case may be delayed. Delayed?! It had already been over eight months!

Finally, another Department of Veteran's Affairs document dated February 5th, 2015 arrived. It stated that John was granted a monthly VA pension based upon his incompetency. I signed papers with Mr. Welles appointing me as John's fiduciary representative. John finally began receiving a monthly VA pension check directly deposited into his own checking account that I had opened for him. A set amount of his monthly pension was to go to his wife as aid and attendance money, to be used for her care.

John in England, c.1943

CHAPTER 9

The Fallout of D-Day Continues

THE STATE OF flux that John and Mary were experiencing since August 1ˢᵗ was about to become even worse and more complicated. The events in this chapter will help you better understand what constant change means in a healthcare setting that involves health insurance, Medicaid, and nursing homes.

Mary's Hospitalizations Continue

After returning to River's Edge in a coma on August 22ⁿᵈ, Mary slowly became a little stronger, but more forgetful than before her mini-stroke. She had no recollection of going to St. Bernadette's emergency room on August 22ⁿᵈ. She kept saying that she just wanted to go home to live again. The county CASA agency came to River's

Edge and evaluated her on September 3rd, and presented her with realistic options for all possibilities; both living at home with regular home health nursing visitations, and also with what's involved if she needed to be admitted to a nursing home. I applied for Medicaid for her on August 29th, thinking that the skilled nursing level in a nursing home was probably where she was headed. Her Medicare HMO Advantage Plan health insurance informed her that their coverage for her expenses at River's Edge would end on September 7th, so the River's Edge Medicaid coordinator classified her as "Medicaid Pending" at that point.

Mary continued to be depressed over all that was going on in their lives now. What follows is the letter that Mary wrote to her sister-in-law Ginny (John's brother Ronnie's wife) in Massachusetts in early September 2014:

> *Dear Ginny, Well our life is changed. John is living at Sunrise Knoll in Johnson City and I am living at River's Edge in Binghamton. We couldn't get a place together, no room available. I'm on his list but no luck as yet. John's dementia is not too bad but I had to be put in the hospital and could not leave him home alone. I stayed in the hospital two weeks, and so far here I've been here three weeks. I don't know how long much longer. I fall down all*

the time & can't & can't get up. I am 89 years
old. I miss my regular life. Love, Mary

Mary kept complaining of increased abdominal pain during early November. The nurses at River's Edge kept giving her acetaminophen and telling her that it was just a belly ache. Mary asked to go to the hospital because the pain was quite bad, but her nurses dismissed it and told her, "You want to go to the hospital for a belly ache?"

On Tuesday, November 11th, Pat checked in on Mary and immediately could see that this was more than a "belly ache." Once again, as she did in August, Pat summoned NP Connie Juliet, who examined Mary and said that she needs to go to the ER immediately. On the drive to St. Bernadette's emergency room, the ambulance EMT's didn't like the look of her EKG so they diverted the ambulance to Staunton General in Johnson City, since it was known for its cardiac care—just in case.

In Staunton's ER, Mary had tests that diagnosed an inflamed gall bladder in addition to her liver abscesses flaring up. She was admitted, and in two days she had surgery to remove her gall bladder, spending time in the intensive care unit after surgery. The hospitalizations of John and Mary were almost becoming a daily routine! John went to St. Bernadette's ER on November 6th and again on the day before Mary's gall bladder surgery. We were all numb and mentally exhausted from dealing with hospital visits and surgeries for both of them, in addition to the paperwork involving Medicaid applications and health insurance claims and cancellations. To make matters worse, Mary contracted a *C. diff.* infection while an inpatient at Staunton General, and was placed in an isolated room. Anyone visiting her had to wear gloves, a mask, and a disposable gown.

(*Clostridium difficile*, often called *C. diff*, is a bacterial infection that can cause symptoms ranging from diarrhea to life-threatening inflammation of the colon. Illness from *C. diff.* most commonly affects older adults in hospitals or in long-term care facilities and typically occurs after use of antibiotic medications.)

Mary was an inpatient at Staunton General from Tuesday November 11th until Monday December 1st, one day short of three weeks. Things were about to change drastically however—very soon.

———∞———

"Although the world is full of suffering, it is also full of the overcoming of it"

- Helen Keller, American educator who overcame the adversity of being blind and deaf to become one of the 20th century's leading humanitarians

Miracles, Hospital Visits, and Moving

While Mary was in rehab at River's Edge and John in the dementia unit at Sunrise Knoll, one of the four care-takers would either bring Mary to see John, or John to see Mary for a visit. Mary was already feeling depressed about her situation at River's Edge, and visiting John at Sunrise Knoll likely made her feel even worse, as his living conditions were vastly superior to hers. I know her visits to see John made her feel even more adamant to leave River's Edge, but at the moment she was still in the hospital battling her *C. diff.* infection.

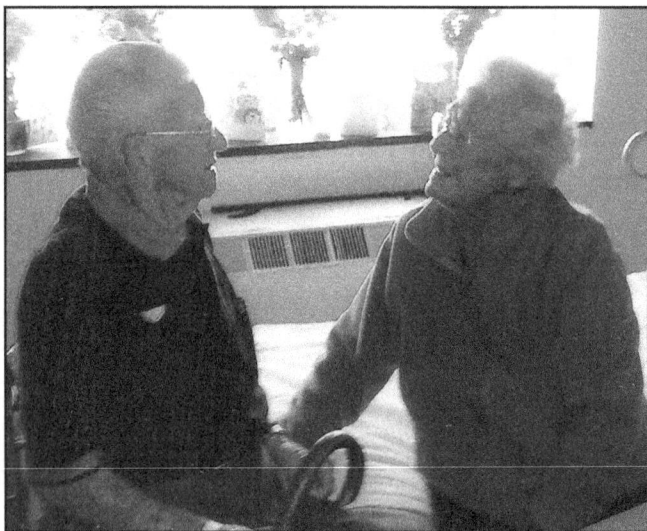

John visits Mary, August 29, 2014

On Tuesday evening, November 18th, Marge called

me. She had been in discussions with Unified Christian Communities (UCC) admissions people, and I'm quite certain that she made a good case for being able to allow Mary and John to live in the same facility. Whether it was the CEO of UCC, or someone on her staff, Marge told me that they were making Mary a bed offer! The offer was being made for Mary to share the room with John at Islington House, even though it was on a dementia unit. Would she want such an arrangement? Marge was as stunned as I was that an offer was being extended, as Mary and John were definitely under the monetary limits that UCC typically requires to offer admission. Someone was smiling down upon them to be sure!

Since John was moving to a semi-private 2-bed room at Islington House's dementia unit the next day, November 19th, Mary would be allowed to have the other bed in that room if such an arrangement would be acceptable to her (remember that Islington House and Westmoor Hall are a part of the same parent company, UCC). She was in the middle of her hospital stay treating a *C. diff.* infection, but when she was well enough to be discharged, she could be moved directly from Staunton General Hospital to Islington House if she accepted.

Mary and John's moves were bad timing for Pat and me, because we had recently bought a ranch style home. One-floor living gave Pat minimal need to go up and down stairs, which were becoming increasingly more difficult since receiving intense chemotherapy for lymphoma in 2005. That chemotherapy left her with severe neuropathy in her legs. I spent all my spare moments at the new home during October and early November, painting and remodeling. We had the movers load all of our belongings from our 2-story home on November 18th, ready to move it into our new ranch home on November 19th. We spent the night at a local motel—exhausted from the day's packing. On the morning of the 19th, I went to our new home to spend the day directing the movers where to put things, while Pat went to Sunrise Knoll to sign all the paperwork required for John's transfer to Islington House.

Mary accepted the offer of the room at Islington House, knowing that she would be living with John, but on a dementia floor. She was well enough to be discharged from the hospital on December 1st. As Pat was making arrangements to have her transferred to Islington House, Kathy went to River's Edge to empty Mary's room of her belongings and take them to Islington House. The staff at River's Edge asked Kathy what she was doing, to which she replied, "Mary's not coming back here."

The reunion for John and Mary was short lived. Two

days after Mary's arrival on December 1st, 2014, John fell in their room and severely cut the back of his head, requiring yet another visit to St. Bernadette's emergency room. John had a CT scan, they stitched the back of his head, and he spent the night for observation as an inpatient. When he returned, Mary would carefully follow the instructions given to her and gently clean the back of John's head. Less than one week after John had fallen, Mary was taken to the Staunton General emergency room again with her second *C. diff.* flare up. She was admitted into isolation once again, meaning that we had to gown and glove up, and wear a face mask when visiting her.

If that wasn't enough, the day after Mary returned to the hospital, John fell yet again, requiring another visit to the emergency room. Fortunately, this fall was minor and he returned the same day. This routine of constant hospital visits for the two of them got to the point where we felt like we could just drive to one hospital or the other on any given day and find one or both of them in that hospital being treated for something! It was both physically and emotionally exhausting.

Together Again, Sort Of

Both John and Mary eventually returned to their 2-bed room on Islington House's third floor. In January 2015,

I divided their available cash in their joint checking account, giving each of them their own checking account. This was necessary in order to keep their assets separate, as each of them had limitations imposed by Medicaid. By February 2015, less than three months after he had arrived at Islington House, John was officially designated chronic Medicaid eligible.

Mary was slowly improving physically, but it was obvious that she was still mentally depressed. Between caregiver burnout that began sometime in 2014, her sudden bouts with various severe illnesses, and her bad experiences at River's Edge, she was feeling pretty low. As much as she was very happy to be together with John again and able to watch over him, living on a dementia unit was not helping her to socialize in any way. There literally was no one on the floor with whom to carry on a normal conversation. She was not demented, and it was taking its toll on her. Her days were spent either helping John for a while or watching a lot of television in her room while curled up in a small, pink recliner and rocker that we bought her to use in her new home. LPN Annie told me that Mary was so depressed over being surrounded by demented people that she pleaded with her to help her move.

Mary told her, "I'm little, put me in your car trunk and take me out of here. I'm going nuts."

Mary told me, "I can't talk with anybody. They're all in their own world." She kept insisting that she was able to return home to live. In her mind, she could still function independently. Try as we all did, she was adamant about leaving the dementia unit and returning home.

Marge saw in Mary a caregiver already near burnout in April of 2014, four months before the D-Day crisis changed everything. Marge could see that the stamina Mary needed to help care for John back in April of 2014 was compromised by her own chronic pain and fatigue. There was no respite from constantly supervising John's daily whereabouts and safety. That's why Marge gave a recommendation for hiring an in-home caregiver on a limited schedule to help with transportation, house cleaning, personal care and more. The reason for that recommendation was not only to provide better care for John, but also to give Mary some badly needed rest from caregiving herself. Had she done that, Mary would have had some time to enjoy whatever helped her to relax, rather than constantly addressing the next need. My feeling as to why she didn't follow through on that recommendation was because Mary was raised by parents who were from the old country school, meaning you just bear down and do it yourself. Mary was raised during the Great Depression of the 1930s, and never forgot how hard it was to save money required for basic needs. Mary grew up with that mindset. Then when she and John first married, money again was an issue for years, and that only added to the mindset that saving money was very important. Because that mindset was a way of life for the first 45 years of Mary's life, it was nearly impossible to change that thought process.

During early January 2015, Pat and I discussed Mary's situation at length. Pat spent over thirty years as a registered nurse, most of those years in various nursing and supervisory roles in nursing homes, so her mom's story was not unfamiliar to her. Pat's professional assessment was that her mom would either be best served in assisted living or adult care, and we made Mary's social worker at Islington House, Frida Tretow, aware of that. What follows are excerpts of a letter I gave to Frida on January 12th, 2015, telling her what our feelings were concerning Mary going back home to live.

Mary Sedlak is a strong-willed woman who needs to be in control of her surroundings. She doesn't want anyone controlling her life. It's her nature. The events that have happened to her and John since August 2014 have overwhelmed her and likely left her with clinical depression. There is daily crying, fits of rage, and her wishing she would die. She has serious heart and GI tract issues, her right knee has reduced her to using a rollator to get around, and her stroke in late August has made her lifelong, headstrong judgment less than sharp. She forgets or doesn't remember some important things, and is now more easily confused. Contrary to Mary's beliefs, the reasons her family doesn't want her to go home are simple—a myriad of safety and social issues. All we want is for her to be safe, comfortable, around people, and cared for—and out of the hospital.

On Going Home

Safety Issues – *Mary will be living on frozen food and candy, as she won't cook much, if at all. She told us so. Her laundry is in the basement. She is adamant about buying another car, but has serious issues with her hearing and vision. She needs a rollator or walker just to get to the car. She will undoubtedly attempt going both up and down the stairs inside and outside her house. Therefore ramps are likely needed outside and chairlifts are needed inside. Those items are a significant added expense. In assisted living Mary has all she medically needs right outside her door. If living at home, she would need transportation to go to appointments, to get medicines, etc. When she falls again, it will be a 9-1-1 call, the ER, and "another "Medicaid Nursing Home—bringing us back to August 1st, 2014 all over again.*

Social Issues – *In assisted living Mary will have people* *all around her, and activities—which is what she needs. Her chief complaint now is "nothing to do." At home she will have no one 98% of the time, the exact thing she does not need. In addition, John will deteriorate further and faster if she moves away, whether he can vocalize it now or not. They've wanted to be together, and Mary living on the same campus as John would keep them together far more than if she were to move back home. Living at home would have Mary concerning herself with every aspect of property and household maintenance and upkeep, the last thing she needs to concern herself with now.*

The old saying "the grass is always greener on the other side of the fence" has Mary's mind painting living at home a bright green, all because she has nothing to do. In reality, for all the reasons I've outlined and more, she doesn't realize how "good" she can have it at Westmoor Hall, if she could only understand all that's just been said here. She needs to be made to understand all the consequences of moving home vs. assisted living. If she could only realize that we're all on her side, both family and caregivers at the Unified Christian Communities campus.

After several telephone calls with Frida, she and her staff agreed that Mary should be given the opportunity to move to the other building on the UCC campus, Westmoor Hall, in a private room in the adult care wing. Islington House and Westmoor Hall are connected below ground by a tunnel that is used by both residents and staff. This meant that in inclement weather, Mary could use her rollator walker and visit John without having to go outdoors. Mary moved to her new private room in adult care on January 15th, 2015; six weeks and three days after arriving at Islington House.

Medicaid And Finances—Again

I met with elder care attorney Priscilla Mason again, this time on January 23rd, to go over all of the changes taking place. She told me not to put their house up for sale until John was officially on Medicaid (which occurred on February 1st, a little over a week after our meeting). Once he was on Medicaid, I should transfer ownership back to Mary and put it on the market. It was frustrating, but necessary to transfer ownership of their home twice in less than six months, and we soon made Mary the sole owner of their home. The constantly changing health status for each of them necessitated these two ownership transfers, which cost John and Mary a total of $1,200.

With Mary moving to Adult Care, and John now on Medicaid, Mary's Medicaid status had to change. She lost her nursing home Medicaid status and needed to be transferred to Community Medicaid instead. This change occurred on February 15th, 2015.

Mary and John both had prepaid burial accounts already in place, but they were not irrevocable, so I contacted the funeral home director Mr. Felix Slade in early February 2015, and he changed both accounts to irrevocable status. Once irrevocable, Medicaid could no longer count that money as an asset.

On March 30th, 2015, we placed their lifelong home for sale on the real estate market. Kathy and Rick took on the responsibility of cleaning out their entire house, selling larger pieces of furniture, kitchen items, and clothing, and placing the money from these sales into Mary's account. Mary kept an end table, an orange living room chair, and her small desk that she used at home to write out all the household bills. I moved them to her private room at Westmoor Hall in February of 2015. The house sold quickly as it was in good condition, having been well maintained over the sixty-six years that John and Mary lived there. The closing took place on May 29th, 2015.

On May 5th, shortly before the closing, I met again with Priscilla Mason to make sure that we all understood what was about to happen once the money from the sale was received. At the closing, Medicaid was reimbursed almost $11,000 from the sale proceeds since it had already paid some nursing home expenses. That money was granted with the understanding that the county would file a Real Property Tax Lien to recoup as much as possible of the expenses paid out when the house was sold. The remaining money put Mary's assets above what Community Medicaid would allow, so she became a private pay resident at Westmoor Hall. Once she spent down her assets, she would be able to re-apply for Medicaid.

Mary Adjusts To Adult Care Living

Mary's roller coaster changes in her health status were happening on a weekly basis, so long term planning for her was impossible to do. As of mid-January 2015, she had fluctuated between living at home to seriously ill (several times) and living in a skilled nursing rehabilitation stay at a nursing home. And all this in less than six months.

Once she entered the adult care wing at Westmoor Hall, she finally had her own first floor room again; a room that looked and felt more like a hotel room rather than a hospital room. She had her own desk, chair, and end table from home, and she began caring for a few small floral pots that she kept on her east-facing window ledge. She had Pat and I buy her several scented candles, and we also bought her a small refrigerator to keep things cold. The dining room was almost directly across the hall, making it a short walk without causing a lot of leg pain. She could take the nearby elevator to the ground floor and slowly walk through the tunnel to visit John whenever she wished to—and she did. In adult care, Mary had a wonderful Licensed Practical Nurse (LPN), Jessica, that helped her with all of her daily medications. She brought them on time every day and made sure that Mary had everything that she needed. The maintenance crew always made sure that mirrors and pictures were hung properly, and were quick to respond to any issues that arose.

Despite all of the assistance and a wonderful room, Mary was becoming bored—again. She told me that she felt too confined and bored with the routine of eating in the dining room and coming back to her room and napping away the hours lying on her bed. Going to see John was fine for her (although a bit of a walk through the tunnel), but after a short time with him, her issues with trying to adapt to *their world* of cold stares and unintelligible speech surfaced, and she had to return to her reality. On more than one occasion she told me that she simply wished to die, which I always relayed to her new social worker at Westmoor Hall, Gina Navarro.

Mary was a cigarette smoker, a habit she acquired after she and John married. Since the UCC campus was smoke free, Mary had to go off grounds to smoke. During her brief time living at Islington House with John, she would walk to a nearby picnic table located on the grounds of a gas station located right next to Islington House. She would often smoke together with nurses and other UCC staff members who also smoked. Once she moved to adult care at Westmoor Hall, the gas station was farther away, making the walk harder on her. She never smoked a great deal, but the need to walk farther to smoke, especially in colder weather, made the situation all the more difficult. That, plus her increasing depression, led Mary to try and occasionally sneak a cigarette in her bathroom. She thought that no one would find out, but the smell of cigarette smoke travels readily throughout a smoke free building, and she was soon reported. Gina confronted me with the story before they spoke to Mary. She told me that they all love Mary and did not want to jeopardize her residency, but if she continued to smoke after she was warned, they would have no choice but to dismiss her. Common sense prevailed and Mary had to suffer through the longer walks outdoors so as to be able to smoke.

Whether it was depression taking over her thoughts, or illness setting in once more, on March 1st, 2015, Mary was again transported by medi-van and admitted to Staunton General with—you guessed it—her third *C. diff.* infection. Fortunately this infection was not as severe as the previous ones, so she was able to return to Westmoor Hall in several days' time. Once back in her room, her desire to return back home to live became a part of her daily conversation again, perhaps because she knew that the financial realities of her situation were pointing to the need to sell their home soon. As you've already read, their home was listed for sale less than a month later, March 30th.

Mary Adjusts To Independent Living

The financial necessity of selling their house had to take precedence over Mary's desire to live at home again. She was spending down her money regularly, and would run out of money in the near future if nothing was done. In late May of 2015, Mary's social worker Gina began to look for any available apartments in the independent living wing at Westmoor Hall, as Mary's physical health seemed to be improving enough to warrant a move to independent living. None were available at the time, but two were scheduled to become available in about three weeks. Gina took Mary to see them both in mid-June. One was on the ground floor and the other on the second floor. The second floor apartment was quite spacious, with an open living room and kitchenette layout, a large walk-in closet with a door, a good-sized bedroom with a closet and a bathroom with a walk-in shower off the bedroom. The kitchenette included a small refrigerator and a microwave oven. Facing west, next to the living room window, was a door leading out to a balcony that overlooked a wooded area and a view of a neighboring pond. Her balcony was on the rear side of Westmoor Hall away from street traffic, so it was very quiet with a picturesque view.

Mary liked the second floor apartment. After they cleaned and re-painted it, she moved in on July 10th, 2015. They brought over her desk, chair, end table, and television from her adult care room, but she needed some additional furniture now that the furniture from her house had been sold. I took her to a local home furnishings store one afternoon, and she selected a single bed and mattress, a dresser, a 2-seat couch, and a small table and chair for the kitchenette.

In addition to being pleased with her new apartment, Mary also liked the fact that the monthly rent for it was less than half that of a month's rent in adult care. She was now in independent living, not adult care, so there was no nursing supervision. Mary was very afraid of spending down to the point in which her remaining money would dwindle down to where she'd be forced to move into a semi-private room in adult care, so saving as much as she could was foremost in her mind.

Her overall health status had improved somewhat, but she still had serious health issues with stage 3 kidney failure, liver abscesses, a heart condition, a bad right knee, and some hearing loss. The four caretakers (Pat, myself, Kathy, and Rick) felt that she should remain in adult care because of all these health issues, but Mary was forever "the energizer bunny." She just kept going and going despite the odds against her. It was remarkable to see how she bounced back from her very serious health issues that came to a head in August 2014, but what was even more remarkable was about to happen very soon.

The Energizer Bunny Gets Wheels

After a month of independent living , Mary really enjoyed her new apartment. It was a longer walk to go and visit with John but she managed, often using a cigarette break along the way to break up the walk. Mary had a regular meal schedule in Westmoor Hall's dining room, just as she did when she lived in adult care. The problem was Mary wasn't fond of much of the food they served. She always said that the ladies who sat at her assigned dining room table with her would eat anything, but she had issues with food taste and texture, making it hard to swallow. She would always ask us to stop and pick up some groceries for her when she knew one of us was coming over. She had a small refrigerator, so she could keep milk on hand and have cereal for breakfast instead of going to the dining room. She bought a toaster so she could make toast. Mary was no longer an early riser like she was in her working days. Long standing habits are hard to change, so waking up and getting dressed for an early breakfast was not easy for her.

Many times that summer of 2015, we'd all hear how we sold her car without her permission. The fact that she was at death's door when we did that didn't seem to matter. She kept telling us that she's better now and wants a car to be able to go to the store or a Bingo game without having to bother one of us all the time. We were all opposed to the idea because of her issues with eyesight and significant hearing loss, but Mary was persistent. She made calls to several car dealerships to find out about prices for a used car, and calls to insurance companies to check on auto insurance rates. She finally bought a 2010 Chevrolet Cobalt in late September 2015. I took her to buy car insurance, and the dealer helped her to get a new set of license plates.

Less than two weeks after she bought the car, she was taken to Staunton General for her fourth *C. diff.* infection. This one was serious, so they admitted her into an isolated area as in her earlier episodes with *C. diff.* She was in the hospital for almost a week before she was discharged.

Once back at Westmoor Hall, she began driving again. She'd go out to an afternoon Bingo game now and then, and also out for a few groceries. One other asset of having her own car was that Mary would now drive, rather than walk, to visit John in the next building. It made it much easier on her chronic knee pain to not have to walk that distance. She kept one rollator in the car trunk to be used whenever she was out with her car. Another big asset for her was that she could now take the elevator from her second floor apartment to the basement, walk out a short distance to her parked car, and smoke her cigarette. It was much closer than going to the gas station on the other side of Islington House, and in inclement weather she could stay warm and dry in her car when she smoked.

Although we were all still worried about the driving with all of her health issues that could lead to an auto accident (she never drives in the dark), she continued to amaze us with her determination to remain independent for as long as she could. Her white Chevy Cobalt had a few minor dings and several of the hubcaps were now cracked from hitting a curb too hard, but Mary, the energizer bunny, had wheels.

CHAPTER 10

Life in Their World

Sunday Dinner on the Third Floor

The elevator door opened and I walked onto the third floor vestibule at Islington House. I pressed the automatic door opener for the double doors to gain entry to the dementia unit. I was now in *their world*. Loretta, a resident, was slowly shuffling past as the doors opened, so I had to wait until they closed before I walked down the hall, otherwise she might have tried to "escape," as she was prone to do. Loretta and I were both officers in a local ethnic heritage club some years ago, and I remember her as smart, inquisitive, and more than willing to voice her opinion. She came to Islington House from Sunrise Knoll at the same time as John, as both were no longer able to function well at the assisted living level. LPN Annie beamed a smile and said "hi" as she went running by. She usually had twelve things to do at once, so she seldom walked anywhere. As I walked down the hallway, a cleaning lady came out of Ellie's room with a rolled up pile of soiled linens. When I got to the dining room entry, I could see that my father-in-law, John, was already seated, waiting for lunch. Millie was sitting next to him. They seat four to a round table in the dining room, but John and Millie were the only two sitting at his table today. He didn't see me yet, but I could see that he did not have his upper denture in, so I kept walking down the hall to his room to see where it might be. As I neared John's room, I could hear Wally in the room next to his. In his day, Wally was one of the best tool and model makers at IBM. He made many an intricate model for me when I was a mechanical engineer at IBM in what I call life #1, before I saw the handwriting on the wall and re-careered into a male dental hygienist over twenty years ago. As I peeked into Wally's room, I saw him in his usual pose, curled up on his bed, half covered with his blanket. He was praying to his sweet Jesus, but interspersing his repetitive prayer with moans, asking for someone to help him. This incessant ritual of his continued. Wally's wife had passed away a few years earlier, and my guess was that put him over the limit of what he could bear.

I went into John's room and opened the bathroom door. His denture cup was on the small shelf alongside his sink, so I put on a pair of vinyl gloves to begin cleaning them before I took them with me to the dining room to insert them for John. Upon opening the cup however, I could see that the back corner on the right side of his denture was broken off, and the left corner had a fracture line in it. So much for eating with an upper denture for the next several weeks! I walked down to the nursing supervisor's office and found her at her desk going over reports. I asked her if she knew that John's denture was broken. She did not, but would ask Annie, the LPN on duty if she did. I explained that they would need to be sent out for repair, if they were even repairable. After I thought it over, I decided to take them to my very good friend and office dental technician, Chris Claus, instead. Chris expertly repaired them within one day.

After that short visit, I went to the dining room and pulled up a chair next to John so I could help feed him his Sunday noon pureed dinner. He said "Hi Nick," as he fidgeted with his terrycloth bib, still on the table. He asked me if I had worked today, as he does at every visit. I told him yes, even though it was Sunday. In his mind I knew that John was still fighting World War 2, having served in the 466th Bomb Group in the Eighth Air Force in Attlebridge, England. Just a week earlier at the unit's Christmas Party, Santa spent some time with all the residents. After he left John to visit the others, John leaned over to me and asked, "Is he a Nazi?"

141

His table mate Millie was staring at me in her usual, stoic way, never saying anything. I smiled and waved at her, which brought out a weak, half smile, then back to her usual stone-faced stare. Soon after, her lips opened as if she was speaking, and I could see a few front teeth, but I heard nothing. Millie was mouthing some words, but made no sound. I took John's bib and tied it around his neck while he mumbled some words to me that sounded like words I knew, but spoken in no logical order; before ending his rambling with "good job." Loretta, who I had seen slowly pushing her walker when I first came on the unit, walked by our table, but this time she was pushing a dining room chair. Millie kept playing with an empty soda can she had just finished drinking as Loretta walked out through the dining room entry arch with the chair. Soon after, I saw a certified nursing assistant (CNA) come running into the dining room loudly asking the other aides if they knew where Loretta's walker was. Sandy, a short, well dressed CNA said, "There it is," as she pointed across the dining room toward the other entry. All the while, Loretta kept yelling out, "I want to go home." Loretta's voice has changed over the years; now having a distinct nasal quality to it. Her words now came out sounding much like those spoken by a severely hearing impaired person.

Judy, a resident at the next table, threw a weak smile my way. Judy and John often sat together in the lounge area during the day, and in their own way, they communicated with each other. I saw it clearly at that moment, because Judy was sticking her tongue out at John. Once I made John aware that Judy was "signaling" him, he saw, and returned her gesture by sticking out his tongue too. Then Judy placed her right thumb on the tip of her nose and began to wave her remaining fingers at John. He wasted no time in returning that gesture as well. I'm sure that he had done this with her many times as they whiled away the hours in the lounge, and it was now obvious that Judy was a quick study. I met her many years ago when she was a nursing supervisor at a dementia unit in another local nursing home. She had now come full circle, herself afflicted with the dreaded disease with which she used to help others live. About a year earlier, when Judy was more coherent, she whispered to me, "I used to run one of these places, now I live in one." When Pat began her geriatric nursing career, she worked with and for Judy. Pat always said that Judy was a terrific nurse.

Stan, a temporary male CNA, wheeled Vera to our table from her room. She looked very confused, as she used to sit at table#5 with John, but was moved to another table a few months ago. Stan obviously didn't know. Vera waved and smiled as I directed Stan to the correct table. I remember talking with Vera often when she used to sit next to John. She invited me to her room one day after dinner to show me the gallery of her paintings hanging on her wall. As I looked at them, I immediately saw that she was not simply a hobby painter. Vera was a terrific artist. Her oil paintings were magnificent works of art. One of her paintings was a portrait of Jesus that had become such a favorite among her family and friends, that she had hundreds of copies printed to give out as gifts. She still had her paints and brushes on a nearby shelf. When I told her that she should continue painting, she simply replied, "I can't anymore." Vera used to fall asleep quite often when at the dinner table. She would feel terrible if she knew I saw her upper denture come halfway out of her mouth every time she did that. Vera is a gem of a lady.

Several tables away from us, CNA Phyllis was trying to get resident Ben to sit down, as dinner was being brought around: pot roast with gravy, mashed potatoes, and a San Francisco blend of vegetables. Ben waved his arms around as he asked, "Why do I have to sit down?" Phyllis replied, "Because it's time to eat lunch." Ben immediately followed with, "I'm not ready yet," to which Phyllis repeated her request to have him sit. Ben then blared out, "I'll give you the finger!" as he raised his right hand and finger high in the gesture that his words implied. Phyllis controlled her laughter as she tried to calm him down, but Ben then blurted out "I'll give you the finger again!" along with the gesture; this time with both hands. Millie just stared into space, as if in a trance, and John just kept fidgeting with his bib, endlessly wiping the table clear of some imaginary mess that only he could see; while Loretta kept screaming that she wanted to go home. Millie finally knocked the empty soda can on the floor. That was it for her. She used her legs to maneuver her wheelchair away from the table and out of the dining room; her full plate of food sitting there, untouched. Frank, another resident at the table across the aisle yelled out "Shit" in frustration as he could not reach the glass of cranberry juice he had just knocked off the table and spilled beneath his wheelchair.

Sunday dinner in *their world* was underway, and all the characters were in good form.

—◦◦◦—

The best to the nurses, aides, and entire staff who keep all the residents safe and well cared for in their world.

—◦◦◦—

More Mealtime Memories

I came onto the third floor and entered *their world* at about 11:45 that Monday morning. As I strolled down the hall toward the lounge area, LPN Annie ran past me as she shouted "hi" in her usual smiling, but very busy way. Next, I ran into Don, walking his wife Lillian down the hallway, as he often does. Don comes to feed Lillian (who is a resident) almost every day. I often see him in the dining room several tables over from John, carefully and lovingly feeding Lillian. As I walked past the two of them, I said hi, and Lillian immediately smiled and said, "Hi, who are you?"

Don explained that she has this same reply to everyone. Lillian was a resident on John's floor at Sunrise Ridge a little over a year before. She, Loretta, and John "graduated" to the skilled nursing dementia unit within weeks of one another.

I found John asleep in one of the lounge recliners, his full upper denture resting on his chin near the top of his shirt. Most of the residents were already in the dining room nearby, but since John was quite tired that morning the staff let him get a few more minutes of sleep. The large screen television in the lounge was playing an old Red Skelton movie, so I sat in the recliner next to John and watched a few minutes of it. Before long, CNA Phyllis came by to wake John and take him to the dining room. Phyllis was shaking him and moving his arms, but John was still fast asleep. She finally whispered in his ear, "John John, let's get ready to go, it's time for lunch," as she hugged him and kissed his forehead.

He slowly started to come around, but very slowly. Phyllis finally got him sitting up in the lounge chair. He was still groggy, with eyes barely half open, but he cast a smile my way as she and I helped him get to his feet and grab hold of his walker. As Phyllis was holding him, she guided him and his walker to table number five in the dining room.

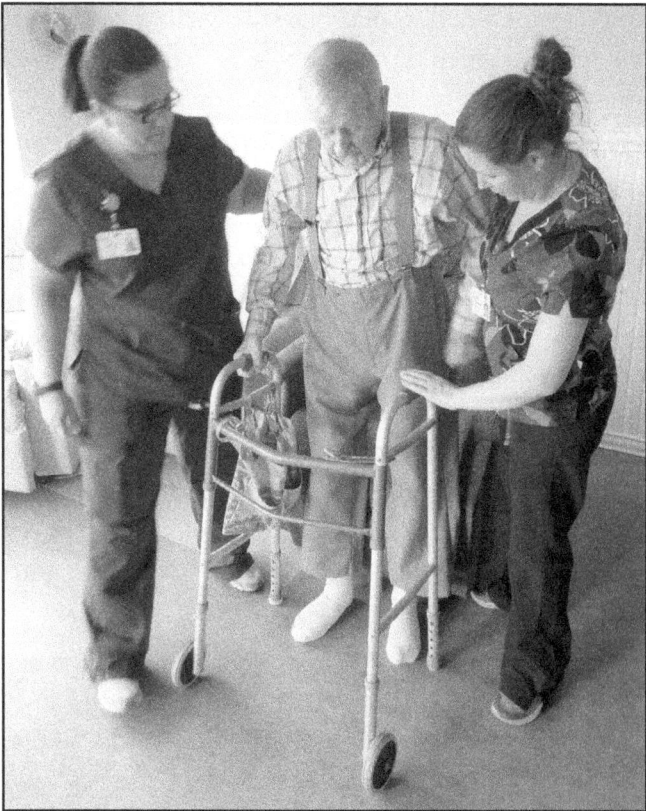

Helping John up for lunch, March 2017

John had the usual two ladies at his table that day. Across from him sat Millie in her wheelchair, expressionless as always. She had before her a nice lunch that included chicken cacciatore, buttered noodles, and green peas. Since Millie usually doesn't eat much at all, they also brought her a peanut butter and jelly sandwich on white bread in case the main course wasn't to her liking. Her meal sat there, untouched through the entire lunch hour, as Millie just slept in her wheelchair slumped to one side. Next to John was Betty, a newer resident who had only been there a month or so. She quietly chatters away, but seldom makes any real sense. Today was no exception. When her meal came, she proceeded to cut her food, and cut it, and cut it yet again. She took twenty minutes to finish cutting all that was on her plate, then proceeded to eat slowly. She began eating her tossed salad with her hands as she always did. Once she went to her main course, she used her butter knife to try and eat it! She used nothing but her butter knife for the entire meal, having the hardest time with the green peas. She managed to get two or three peas on the knife blade as she maneuvered the knife into her mouth, trying to let the peas roll down the knife blade.

John finally was awake enough to eat, so I began to give him spoonfuls of pureed chicken cacciatore, which he readily took. He must have been quite hungry that day, because after only a few moments of my feeding him, he took the nearby fork and began to scoop up small amounts of his pureed lunch (a brown pile, a green pile, and an off white pile) and guide them slowly into his mouth. He kept this up for most of the lunch, although he had a hard time keeping very much food on his fork each time he scooped it up. His meals were given to him on a scoop plate, which has higher side walls to make it easier for him to get more food on his fork without shoving it off his plate and onto the table. As we were almost finished with the main course, Jimmy (a staff member from dietary who helps deliver food and drink to each resident at their table) told John, "Here 'ya go Johnny," as he handed him his dessert. John had a nice cup of chocolate pudding which I helped him devour. I had to wipe his face with his terrycloth bib, since everything from his nose to his chin was blotched with brown chocolate, even extending over to each ear.

While feeding John, I kept thinking back to many such similar meals when CNA Laverne would feed John as she and I discussed the residents and politics. Laverne was a smart gal. That summer, we'd often trade stories on the ongoing presidential election campaign of 2016. She was so good with John, and I knew that she really cared for him. It only took several minutes of any given meal to see the way she worked with him. You can't make up that genuine caring for your patient. I gave Laverne some history on John and World

War 2 during our meal times together that summer of 2016, and I know it made her relate to him even better than she already did. Laverne was sent to work on the first and second floors just before the November 2016 election, but I still saw her in the hallway every now and then.

Throughout the entire lunch, Loretta kept making laps around the dining room and hallways, using her walker. She apparently thought I was her son, because with each lap she would walk up to me and mumble, "Honey, where is my father?" I would politely tell her that I didn't know, then she would walk away, mumbling some meaningless words as she continued on with her laps.

Ben, the resident who readily gives people the finger, seldom sat for long at his dining room table, and today was no exception. After spending but two or three minutes eating his lunch, he stood up and proceeded to do laps, but not along with Loretta. This meant that we now had two residents walking in large circles around the dining room; Loretta stopping to question me with each lap, while Ben simply did his laps without pause, wearing his pajamas and slippers. Ben did not need a walker.

At a table across the aisle and two tables up from John sat a resident named Stella. Stella was in a wheelchair, but apparently didn't want to be because during the entire lunch hour, she constantly kept standing up, which would set off the buzzer on her alarm pad. CNA Donna, along with most every staff member, were kept busy running over to her to get her to sit down. They would all politely get Stella to sit, whereupon she immediately proceeded to stand once again. It was apparent that she was very unsteady when standing, so it was obvious why she was required to sit on an alarm pad.

As I was getting ready to leave, John blurted out, "I have to take a piss."

"You do?" I replied.

He smiled his gotcha smile at me and said, "No." After I took a few more steps, John gave me one last piece of advice, saying, "Don't let the door hit you in the ass on your way out, OK?"

As I left the floor after lunch, I ran into Don again as we waited for a staff member to punch in the secure code to open the door. He's a nice, quiet man who was obviously very devoted to his Lillian. We chatted as we rode down the elevator, then we went our separate ways.

Most mealtimes in "their world" go much like this one, with the residents all needing different levels of care.

It's a constant effort on the part of every staff member to adapt to this mixture of patient needs in one dining room and give each resident the care and attention unique to them.

Dr. Jekyll and Mr. Hyde Come To Lunch

As I pressed the automatic door opener to gain entry to the third floor and *their world*, I saw only Millie in the east-west hallway leading to John's room. It seemed a bit unusual to be so quiet for a Saturday just before lunch time, but I quickly let it pass. As I waved and said hello to Millie, she just sat in her wheelchair giving me her typical stone-faced, expressionless stare. As I got to the lounge area outside of the dining room, I saw John napping in a regular straight back chair, not his usual recliner, arms folded and legs crossed. I thought of how many times I'd seen him sitting just like this over the years when he lived at home. He could sleep through a thunderstorm. He was wearing his new sneakers that I bought for him several days earlier. His old, black shoes were becoming quite worn and didn't fit as snugly as they once did, so the sneakers would give him better stability, making him less likely to fall.

Across the small hallway leading directly to the dining room sat Betty (one of John's table mates), talking up a storm to another resident but making little sense. Most, but not all of her words were understandable, but Betty grouped them into a series of connected, disjointed phrases that really meant nothing. She seemed visibly agitated today. I said hello to John after I gently nudged him awake from his nap. We exchanged some words about the day and the weather as we looked out the lounge windows at the sunny sky. CNA Nina came over to help John stand up and grab hold of his walker. It was almost lunch time so he needed to head for the dining room.

Nina took John's left arm and placed his hand on his walker handle and said, "Papa, let's go to lunch, OK?" That was all Betty had to hear. She quickly walked over to us and grabbed John's right forearm with both her hands while screaming "Oh no, you're not taking him anywhere!" Startled, Nina tried to calm her down by saying, "Excuse me Betty, excuse me Betty, please let go." Betty immediately unloaded with "I don't have to go anywhere! I don't have to put up with this shit!" She was on a roll now, and I witnessed the following exchange:

Betty: "I know what to do."

Nina: "Please let him go, Betty."

Betty: "I mean to tell you to tell me. I'll tell you one right now, you want another to take in? Well, you can take that guy. I will talk to you!"

153

Nina: "Please let him go Betty."

Betty: "No! I had a thing and I got my andanon! Oh stop it, ya dummy. Jesus Christ, is there something with your thing?"

John was just staring at them both and not saying anything. He had a confused look on his face as he stood upright holding onto his walker.

Nina summoned another CNA to help try and control Betty as LPN Annie was summoned. This allowed us to get John into the dining room and seated at table number five nearest the door to the lounge. By this time, Millie (John's other table mate) was already seated across the table from John—just staring. Nina and the other CNA brought Betty to the dining room and sat her in her usual spot at table number five, but she had clearly not calmed down.

She continued screaming, "What are ya doin', trying like a jerk? Don't you doin' this, I'm not backing this down here. I'm not taking a dive! I am eighty, ninety, eighty myself! No, I don't know white; too busy right here! No, and it's dirt and get right oughta here! Listen to this damn shit! How can you do this, you know what I'm making? Do you like this waiting? I was sick both times, do you know that? And I am, and you know what you did. It's good, it's good, don't start takin' this thing out. What are you doing?"

By this time, Annie had arrived. She took Betty in her wheelchair to the lounge nearby, where she spent the next ten minutes talking with her. We couldn't see or hear what was really being said but it was clear that Betty was doing a lot of listening, as she wasn't moving around like she had been. The entire dining room was so quiet that you could hear a pin drop. God only knows how much, if any, of that tirade the residents could comprehend, but their silence did not mean that they weren't affected by it. That was obvious. At this point, John leaned over to me and said, "Jesus Christ, she's nuts." Millie too had had enough by this point. Even though her facial expression was still its usual stoic self, she appeared agitated as she proceeded to use her legs to get her wheelchair out of the dining room. She parked herself under the archway that separates the lounge area from the dining room, and just sat there with her back to everyone in the dining room.

At the next table over, Judy (the former nursing home supervisor) mouthed to me as she pointed to her friend, John, "Is he alright? Is he alright?" I nodded and mouthed yes in reply. She smiled and nodded. It was wonderful to see that even in her demented state, Judy was still a nurse.

Annie brought Betty back to the dining room. Betty's personality had completely changed. Annie had transformed her from Mr. Hyde to Dr. Jekyll within ten minutes! Annie told me that every time Betty sees a new face on the floor she gets this way, and Nina was a new CNA on duty today. Betty was now smiling and apologetic for being so out of control. Annie cut all her food for her as she kept reassuring Betty that it was alright. Annie then gave her a hug and a kiss on the cheek. Betty proceeded to eat her salad and main course with her fingers, as she usually does.

After I finished helping John eat his lunch, I told him that I had to leave now, but would return soon. He told me, "Don't get lost, OK Doc?"

I bumped into Annie at the doorway to the floor and we talked for three or four minutes before she entered the code into the keypad that opens the secure door. Annie told me that she wished I had been there yesterday when John proudly lifted his leg and told her, "See my new shoes!" He knew that he had new shoes. I'm glad he liked them. I got to my car and wrote some notes to help me write this description of an unusual lunch in *their world* before I left for home.

It takes a special person to work with the elderly in a compassionate, caring way, despite many times having to contend with unbelievable and challenging circumstances. These special people deserve the thanks and gratitude of everyone for their unselfish devotion to their patients and their profession.

Dinner Without Dentures

As I walked down the hallway on an unusually warm Saturday in January, I saw that John was already in the dining room for lunch, even though it was only 11:45 AM. I went straight to his room to search for his upper dentures that had been missing for three days. I went through everything; under the bed, all his clothes drawers, the bathroom storage, every shirt and pant pocket in his closet. No dentures. I then went to the lounge area, thinking that perhaps they fell out of his mouth while he napped in a recliner, then worked their way down beneath the seat cushion. I flipped all the seat cushions on every recliner, then I turned the entire recliner upside down to look on the floor beneath it. As I was on my knees looking beneath the last of the recliners, CNA Donna was coming out of the lounge bathroom, having just finished toileting resident, Judy. She saw me sprawled on the floor and ran toward me screaming "Are you alright?" I immediately looked up and assured her that I had not fallen, I was just looking for John's denture. She was relieved.

Unfortunately for residents in many nursing homes, try as the staff might, it's all too common for residents to lose things like dentures, hearing aids, and eyeglasses. John's lower denture went missing several months earlier. I had dental technician Chris Claus place his name in both his upper and lower dentures, but they never reappeared.

About a month earlier, John's eyeglasses also went missing. Like his dentures, I had his name on them. I had an old pair of mine at home that I knew would fit John, so I took his last eyeglass lens prescription and had lenses made to fit my old frame. He always commented on how he liked his new glasses. It seems odd that for residents that never leave the floor, such items can somehow get lost. One explanation could be that the resident simply tosses the item into the trash can without thinking, not too far-fetched when dealing with a dementia resident. Another possibility is that a smaller item could somehow be flushed down the toilet. During one of his visits to the hospital emergency room while a resident at Sunrise Knoll, you may recall reading that *both* of his hearing aids were *lost*. John began his nursing home life with two hearing aids, an upper and lower denture, and two pairs of eyeglasses. Over the span of a year, all of those necessities had disappeared. He could no longer hear well, eat well, or see well, yet he was still the same happy-go-lucky man he always was. Anyone who wasn't demented that had those losses happen to them would have been understandably infuriated at having lost their ability to hear, eat, and see well.

After my futile search for his dentures, I went into the dining room to help feed John. I found him alone at his assigned table, because I saw Betty leave for a brief outing with her daughter, and Millie was off roaming the hallways in her wheelchair. As I entered the dining room, Millie gave me an insincere hand wave while she motored by into the hallway. John was sitting close to the table eating his pureed spinach and apple salad with his knife. He had more on his face than in his mouth, so I asked him for the knife in exchange for his teaspoon. After I fed him several spoonfuls, he took the spoon and started feeding himself. He finished the salad, then kept constantly playing with his terrycloth bib. He took both his knife and teaspoon, placed them neatly near the end of the bib (which he had spread across the table in front of him), and began rolling them up in the bib. By then, his main meal came, pureed hamburger. I opened a packet of ketchup and swirled it into the hamburger, turning the brown blob into a reddish-brown blob.

John was looking out the window, pointing to the flock of birds flying by, then saying to me "I'd like to live in that house" (the one below the dining room window, a part of the connected Westmoor Hall facility). He then blurted out, "I'm not going anywhere in this place, so what the hell is the difference?" He now stares off into the distance more than he used to. When he spoke today, he constantly searched for the word or phrase to finish his sentence. I'd reply with things like "I know," or "that's OK" to make him feel like I understood where he was going with his thoughts.

CNA Donna wheeled Millie into her spot next to John, but as soon as Donna left to tend to other residents, Millie simply wheeled herself back into the lounge area. This entry and exit routine went on for three tries, until CNA Phyllis brought her back. Millie had a disgusted look on her face as I heard her mutter to herself, "Shit." For some reason, Millie must have finally been hungry enough to eat, because she took her hamburger (not pureed) and took a bite out of it. She kept chewing and chewing, at least thirty or forty chews until she swallowed. Phyllis sat down next to her to help her eat. John pointed to Phyllis and said to me "There's a smart girl."

Phyllis heard, and a huge smile came across her face. She told me how she and John got along well, "perhaps because we're both Slovak" she said. As she worked with Millie, she told me "You know when I'm away for a few days, John misses me. When I return, he always asks me if I'm alright and if everything is OK. I play John's favorite music for him often, and we have a good time just listening to it." As we continued with dinner, John kept looking at Phyllis, then he began to "play music" with his lips; "brrrrup – bup – bup, brrrrup – bup – bup." Phyllis smiled at him as she began using a knife and a fork on the table top, playing a rhythmic pattern along with his lip music. After a while, John got this devilish grin on his face and told me, "Get your money back!" After Phyllis stopped laughing she said, "I guess that means he doesn't think I'm any good."

As John looked around at everyone in the dining room, the assortment of residents in wheelchairs and other special chairs, he said, "Look at all these poor bastards." Then he smiled his edentulous smile at me as he said "Not you, I don't mean you." I too had to smile as I thought 'He's one of those poor bastards, but he's always making the best of his lot in life.' It reminded me of Viktor Frankl's amazing book "Man's Search For Meaning," describing how he spent years in a Nazi concentration camp and survived to become a successful psychiatrist.

As I was getting ready to leave, John said, "Thanks for coming, my friend." He shook my hand as he often does. I took only two or three steps away from his table when he looked at me and said, "Hey Nick, say hello to the old lady, OK?"

I was still smiling at that one when I ran into Phyllis in the hallway and told her what John had just told me. She got a hearty laugh from that one, and said to me, "I love John," as she let me out the secure door.

———∞———

"Forces beyond your control can take away everything you possess except one thing, your freedom to choose how you will respond to the situation."

- Viktor E. Frankl, Austrian psychiatrist and Holocaust survivor

———◯✕◯———

Feeding the Battery Operated Cat

As I walked down the hallway toward the lounge area, I saw John sitting in an upright chair near the dining room entrance. There was an empty chair next to him, and a new resident in the next chair after that. I sat down and greeted John, as he immediately said, "something is in my room." He acted confused, but my attention soon went to my left arm. The new resident lady sitting in the chair next to mine was grabbing on to my left arm and tugging at it. As I glanced at her in amazement, she blew me a kiss and smiled at me. She then told me not to tell her husband that she did this, so I said, "Don't worry, I won't."

She started laughing out loud—very loud. I saw Kathy and Rick as I came into the building that morning, and they told me of a lady sitting near John who suddenly hugged Rick and asked him to marry her. When

Rick introduced his wife, Kathy, the lady acted embarrassed. I knew that I had just met that same lady.

I walked over to nurse Annie who was in the lounge typing information into the nursing computer on her rolling cart. She told me that John's sore on top of his foot had healed and he was again wearing his new sneakers I had bought for him. John kept picking at a scab on the tip of his nose as Annie and I talked so she tried to convince him to stop.

We soon went into the dining room, where Betty was already seated in her chair next to John. On her lap was a battery operated cat that meowed whenever you petted it. Betty kept petting and talking to the cat as we all waited for the meals to be served. Millie sat across from John—just staring into space. As soon as the food came, Betty began to try and spoon feed the battery operated cat, giving it tossed salad covered in orange-colored French salad dressing. Too bad the inventors didn't program this cat to lick its whiskers clean! This cat would be headed for a bath right after lunch. With a disgusted look on her face, Millie just pulled her wheelchair away from the table and left.

Annie soon came over to help Betty to eat since she wasn't eating herself, but rather trying to shove food into the battery operated cat's mouth. The floor around her was covered with lettuce and orange salad dressing and the cat had an orange face, but it was still meowing. Betty said that she thought it liked it and wanted more. Annie and I talked as we both fed our table mates.

John ate most of his pureed chipped beef and biscuits, along with pureed peas. About three quarters through his lunch he clammed up, telling me that he was full. Jimmy the waiter was coming around passing out desserts, and he gave John a small cup of chocolate ice cream. As I gave him his first spoonful he smiled at me and said, "Now that's good."

John kept reaching behind him as if trying to grab onto whatever he thought was there, so I asked him what he was reaching for?"

He looked at me and said, "Something is stuck up my ass," smiling his now big, toothless smile.

Throughout lunch, John kept playing with the far end of his terrycloth bib, folding the ends together, trying to make them stay in place on the table. This made it look somewhat like a terrycloth "bridge" running from his neck to the table. His moving around as I fed him would make the end of the bib on the table fall off, but John kept repeating this ritual throughout the entire meal.

As I was getting ready to leave, I told him that I had to leave but would see him later. He looked at me and replied, "OK, buddy, don't over-rotate yourself." I left, both smiling and shaking my head wondering what he could have meant by that. As I walked toward the secure door, Annie saw me and asked me if I needed someone to help me bust out of the place. I told her I did, and then told her the words John and I just exchanged the minute before. Annie laughed as she headed back to the dining room, telling me she too would try not to over-rotate herself that afternoon.

—⋈—

"It is well known that humor, more than anything else in the human make-up, can afford an aloofness and an ability to rise above any situation, even if only for a few seconds."

- Viktor E. Frankl, Austrian psychiatrist and Holocaust survivor.

—⋈—

Sundowners, and Sleeping Through Dinner

I drove to Islington House on a sunny, cold Saturday late morning to help feed John. Activity Coordinator, Jane Brooks, was the receptionist that day, and she immediately brought up John when she saw me. She told me that she worked with John early last evening and he couldn't sit still. He was restless and constantly moving around, which made it much harder for the staff to keep him from falling. He was experiencing Sundowner's Syndrome, a neurological syndrome where a certain percentage of Alzheimer's patients experience agitation and confusion when the sun goes down. She felt that John needed more activity during the day, as encouraging an active day is one proven method of easing Sundowner's Syndrome.

Every time Jane brought him to a group activity session, he always joins in, so she felt that the increased stimulation during the day might help him be more relaxed during the early evening hours. I thanked her for her concern and told her she really had all of her resident's best interests at heart. She said, "I try. I love all of them."

As I entered the elevator I thought about a study conducted at Purdue University which showed that Alzheimer's patients exhibited significantly more anxiety and wandering during periods of the full moon. I quickly checked and found that the full moon was only one day away. As far as I know, there is no rigid proof that this can occur, but a number of nurses and aides have supported the results of that study over the many years I've discussed it with them.

As I arrived on the third floor it seemed very quiet. When I got to the lounge area I spotted Millie, asleep in her wheelchair near the dining room entryway. I looked around the very quiet lounge area and dining room. Most every resident in both areas seemed to be sleeping. John was sitting in a straight back chair right next to the nurse's station—dozing. His eyes widened some when he saw me. He smiled and touched my hand. After that, he continued to doze. CNA Phyllis soon came over to tell me that John was quite active an hour or so ago. She said that she even toileted him for fifteen minutes, thinking that he may have needed to go to the bathroom, but that wasn't it.

"Active at ten AM?" I replied. "That sounds like Sun-Uppers Syndrome. Maybe his body works on Slovak time" (six hours ahead of eastern time)!

Phyllis laughed. John woke up during this conversation and began telling Phyllis how he was going to do something, but his words only came out as a few incoherent phrases. Phyllis kissed him on the forehead and said, "John, sometimes you're a schmuck," after which they both just laughed and laughed.

When she saw his broad, toothless smile she said, "There's no way I can put a price on how his smile makes me feel."

167

Phyllis then told John that she loved him, to which he replied, "I love you no matter what."

LPN Penny King was covering the west wing of the third floor that day, and Phyllis and Nina were John's CNAs. When Nina came to take John into the dining room, she said, "Papa, are you ready for lunch?"

"Yeah," he said, at the same time raising his right hand and moving it toward Nina. We'll never know, but it appeared that he was trying to grab her breasts. Nina quickly took her ID badge, which was attached to a retractable chain around her neck, and extended it toward him saying, "Do you want to see my badge, John?"

LPN Penny saw this happen and told us what happened the day before as she was getting John ready for lunch. As she was lifting him up to grab onto his walker, he looked at her behind as he was halfway standing and said, "Look at that ass."

Startled, Penny replied, "What did you say?" John let out a big, toothless grin and repeated it. Penny has seen this kind of behavior many times in her career so she simply smiled and went on with her work. She told me that she really likes John. "He's a pip!"

Once in the dining room, Nina sat John into his chair

at table number five. He told her that he built the house seen outside, below his dining room window. Nina told him that he did a good job. Betty wasn't there that day, as she was another of those too tired to come to the dining room. Nina placed her food on a tray and took it to her room. Millie was wheeled in, took one look at her drinks on the table before her, and swatted the coffee mug off the table with one swing of her right hand, spilling coffee everywhere. Millie than wheeled herself back to the lounge.

At the next table, Wally was sleeping in his chair, as was the lady next to him. Penny walked by and asked Wally where his shoes were, as he had none on his feet. "Right where I left 'em," he replied loudly.

John's meal was pureed chipped beef, biscuits, and peas. As I was feeding him he kept talking about his mother forgetting to bring him something. As I fed him each spoonful, he would swallow it and reach for his bib, wiping an imaginary mess off the table.

At one point, Ben went shuffling by the table mumbling some incoherent words. He was taking his usual laps around the dining room during dinner. John watched Ben walk by and then muttered, "Damn fool."

When Jimmy brought John his pureed carrot cake for dessert, John told him that he's a nice guy.

Jimmy smiled and replied," Thanks Johnnycakes, I'm on your side."

John must have been thirsty because he couldn't wait to drink his thickened Cranapple juice. He even took his teaspoon and scooped out the bottom of his glass. After that, he immediately grabbed his thickened glass of milk, but didn't comprehend the fact that it still had a cover on it. He tried to drink it but couldn't figure out why nothing was coming out of his glass. I took the cover off and he thanked me as he began to drink.

As I got ready to leave I told John I'd see him soon. He thought for a minute, processing what I just told him, then smiled at me and said, "OK, Nick, I like having you with me."

The lady cleaning the floors let me out the secure door, and as I arrived in the main lobby, Jane stopped me before I signed out to tell me a story about last night that she forgot to mention when I arrived. As they were doing some group activities, at one point she told John that she loved him. John replied, "I love you too; so, how's your husband?"

It was apparent the John's illness hadn't yet significantly affected his comedic timing!

———∞———

"Avoid arguing or asking for explanations to statements that don't make sense. Plan more active days. A person who rests most of the day is likely to be awake at night. Discourage afternoon napping and plan activities, such as a walk, throughout the day."

- Tips for helping deal with Sundowner's Syndrome, from www.AgingCare.com.

———∞———

John Tries To Leave

I had just come home after a day at the dental office when Pat told me of a phone call that she received shortly before I arrived. She had a serious look on her face. Susie, the third floor charge nurse at Islington House called to tell her that John wasn't doing well at all. He wasn't eating, he vomited several times that day, and he was running a fever. She suggested we come over to see him. Pat called Kathy and Rick and we all met in John's room just after 5:00 PM on a sunny, warm day in August, 2016. Mary was already there sitting with John, who was in bed shaking and twitching uncontrollably in his sleep. He was wearing only underclothes, and was covered with a blanket.

Susie and another nurse had no real update yet, other than telling us that even though he's not awake, he had developed a terrible cough that gurgled a lot. She asked if we wanted him to have a dose of IV antibiotic, or just keep him comfortable. Pat and Susie talked, nurse-to-nurse, then Susie went and came back with a dose of Rocephin IV antibiotic that she gave to John in his butt.

I took Rick for a walk while the women remained in the room with John. He had never met John's dinner table mate, Vera, so we walked down the hall to the south wing of the third floor, and Vera's room. She was there and happily showed Rick her artwork hanging on the walls in her room. Vera was always more than happy to share her paintings with anyone who seemed interested. Rick saw what I did when I first saw her oil paintings—she was a fabulous artist in her day. After we chatted for a while, Rick and I left and returned to John's room.

Susie and the other nursing staff didn't directly say it, but their words to us all indicated that they were very concerned about John. We even went over information about the funeral director who would handle matters when the time came. That August evening gave us every indication that John was preparing to leave. Mary was sitting next to John, holding his hand all the while. She began singing one of his favorite Slovak waltzes to him, "U studánky seděla, do voděnky hleděla (As I sat at the spring, staring into the water)." John just lay there; shaking and twitching uncontrollably. He remained unresponsive. As Mary was singing to him, my thoughts went back to years gone by when the bands that I was a member of played that very song hundreds of times. My mind could see John and Mary on the dance floor, smiling and waltzing together beautifully.

CNA Phyllis was already off shift and driving home when she later told me that a voice inside of her said, "I have to go back and see John." She came back and briefly talked with all of us in John's room. Phyllis felt terrible. After several hours, Kathy, Rick, Pat, and I finally left, as tomorrow was another work day. Mary stayed awhile longer, holding John's hand while sitting at his bedside.

John showed no change the entire next day. We were all preparing for the inevitable. When Pat and I went to see John the following day, we ran into his CNA Phyllis as we were walking down the hall. She seemed excited when she saw us, and told us the following, "I was tending to John in bed this afternoon and decided to play the Slovak music that he and I have listened to in recent months, since I knew he liked it. I turned on

John's cassette player, and as I was washing his legs my eyes caught a glimpse of his arms. He was still in bed, eyes still closed, but he slowly raised both arms and began to conduct the band in tempo with the music he heard!" It was the music he loved throughout his entire life. John was back.

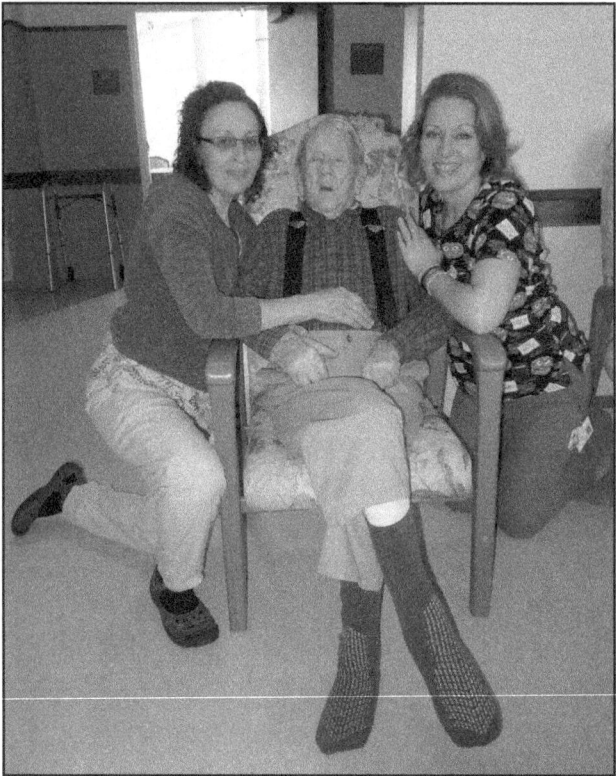

Phyllis and Annie with John in the lounge

———◇✕◇———

"Each night, when I go to sleep, I die. And the next morning, when I wake up, I am reborn."

— Mahatma Gandhi, preeminent leader of the Indian independence movement in British-ruled India.

———◇✕◇———

Mary Hospitalized Yet Again

On Wednesday, March 8th, 2017, Mary came down with the diarrhea and vomiting bug that was running through both Islington House and Westmoor Hall. She was continuously shivering, saying she just couldn't get warm. She remained in her apartment all day. The next day she wasn't any better. We told her to keep drinking plenty of fluids to try and avoid dehydration. On Friday, Mary became very dizzy and fell, pushing the emergency alarm button she wore around her neck. The nurse on duty quickly went to her apartment and saw that Mary had stood up on her own, but she had a slight bruise on her left forearm. The nurse called and told us what had happened, and said that Mary was being sent to St. Bernadette's emergency room for evaluation. She arrived at 1:00 PM and was found to have low blood pressure and dehydration. Pat told the emergency room doctor that Mary had recently been on two different antibiotics: one for a dental extraction, and one for a urinary tract infection. Antibiotics can kill off good bacteria as well as bad bacteria, which can allow *C.diff.* to flourish. She was admitted later that afternoon.

On Saturday, she had a kidney ultrasound which verified her Stage 3 kidney failure we already knew about. We suggested that she be tested for *C. diff.* They agreed, so as soon as they could obtain a stool sample they ran the 48-hour bacterial culture. Over the weekend, she ate very little and was still very cold, covering herself with her outdoor jacket over her hospital blanket. The *C. diff.* test came back positive (her fifth episode in two years), so she was placed in isolation in her room which required all the staff and visitors to wear gowns, masks, and gloves.

Mary developed shortness of breath that was very noticeable when she spoke, so much so that they placed her on oxygen. She was wheezing a great deal and given inhalation therapy for it, along with IV vancomycin antibiotics to treat the *C.diff.*

On Monday, March 14th, Mary spoke with her hospitalist doctor, and then called Pat, telling her, "I've got lung disease (COPD from smoking), kidney disease

(we knew), and heart disease (we knew); don't fret."
She told us that at 91 years of age, she doesn't want
anything done, she just wants to go home to her apartment to die. She told Pat how her hair should be done
for her funeral. I spent time gathering several more
photographs for her funeral to add to those Kathy
and I had put together for the fall of 2014 funeral
preparation.

On Thursday March 16th, Mary awoke in her hospital
bed and later told us, "I looked all around my room.
Everything looked different, yet somehow everything
looked the same. Why am I here?" She still had no
appetite and wasn't eating much, so her doctor felt
that she should be sent to rehab to help her regain
her strength. We suggested that rehab should be at
Islington House rather than another nursing home; as
Mary was quite familiar with it. John was there, and
her apartment was only a building away.

On Friday, Mary called Pat and asked, "What are they
going to do with me?"

Because of Mary's hearing loss, Pat yelled into the telephone, telling her that she'll probably be discharged
from St. Bernadette on Monday. Pat then yelled, "Do
you want me to bring you your heavy jacket?"

"Casket?" Mary asked.

Pat yelled back, "Jacket!"

Mary countered with, "Catheter?"

Mary's hearing had been deteriorating for some time now, so their telephone conversations became quite comical.

On Saturday, Mary's hospitalist physician told her that her lungs were clear now, to which Mary replied, "Bullshit, they're not clear!"

She was right, they weren't. She still had a deep cough and some wheezing. She still had no appetite for anything other than an occasional candy bar.

As if all that had happened in the past four days wasn't enough, Mary mentioned that she no longer had her lower partial denture. I guess it must be a family thing, as both of John's dentures had disappeared under similar circumstances, so why should we be surprised? I wish hospitals and nursing homes would create an effective method that would eliminate most, or all of these losses. Dentures that fit and work properly are expensive, and need to be treated that way. Those people spending down their assets toward an eventual Medicaid existence can ill afford to spend $2,000 to $5,000 for "misplaced" dentures, hearing aids, or eye glasses.

At 1:30 PM on Monday, Mary arrived at the Islington House first floor rehab unit. I noticed that her room-mate wore two hearing aids so I anticipated what was about to happen. Once Mary had her television on, the extreme loudness she required bothered her roommate so much that she just came over to Mary's television re-mote and turned it down. Mary was placed on physical therapy (PT), which she disliked. After two days of PT the therapists already had given her a new nickname: *Mary, Mary, quite contrary.* Mary told them that she'd always been that way. She did well with her walker but her main issue was her long standing problem with her bad knee. She was also having trouble learning how to take her new medicines. One of them was Remeron, an antidepressant and an appetite stimulant. She need-ed both. Her daily meals now consisted of a half bowl of soup and Hershey® bars.

By Wednesday, Mary seemed resigned to the fact that she was unable to properly take her medicines on her own (required of all those living in independent apart-ments). She liked the nurses on ACF from her time spent there a few years ago, and was convinced that she had to give up her apartment and move to ACF again. By the weekend however, the Remeron must have begun to work, as she was more at ease, actually "liked" the food (her appetite was coming back), and felt that she might be able to take her medicines on her own after all.

On Thursday, March 30th, Mary called Pat and *sang* the following, "I'm going home on Monday, I'm going home on Monday!" Her resilience over the years has always been amazing. The energizer bunny had dodged another bullet and was soon returning to her apartment to continue coping with longevity.

CHAPTER 11

Coping with Longevity

WHEN MARY ARRIVED on the third floor, she found John reclined in a lounge chair in the lounge area. He kept trying to get out of the chair, so his alarm pad kept going off. After several such attempts trying to get out of the chair, his CNA took him to the bathroom. After he used the bathroom the CNA brought him back into the lounge, but sat him in an upright chair, not a recliner. He seemed fine after using the bathroom. In all likelihood John needed to use the bathroom but wasn't able to verbalize his need. Instead, he kept doing all he could, which was to keep trying to get out of the chair on his own.

Now sitting in the straight back chair and calm again, he says to Mary, "You're a really nice lady. What's your name?"

Mary said, "I'm Mary Sedlak." John looked inquisitively at her as if trying to interpret and understand what she just said.

Mary followed by saying, "My mother is Justina, and my father is Frank."

John continued to mull this over in his brain, finally coming out with, "I know! Kesa!" (Kesa is Mary's maiden name.) He immediately followed with, "I'm a Presbyterian." After some moments of silence, John looks at Mary and asks, "Where is my wife?"

Mary replies, "I'm your wife, John."

John had that puzzled look as he thought, then asked, "Are you Mary?"

Mary was getting tired and wished to return to her apartment to take a nap, so she asked John if it was OK for her to go home and rest some. John replied, "Oh sure, go right ahead."

Mary slowly stood up, grabbed on to her rollator and headed down the hallway toward the door. She took the elevator down to the main floor of Islington House and outside to her car. She made her one minute drive from one parking lot to the next, parking in her space behind Westmoor Hall. She put her rollator in the trunk of her car and grabbed on to her second rollator that had been sitting outdoors near her parking space. She entered through the rear door and took the elevator to the second floor, slowly walking down the hall to her apartment.

Back at Islington House, Ellen was sitting hunched over on a portable potty chair in the hallway on the third floor. She was trying to have a bowel movement, and kept muttering something about making it happen if they left her alone. As LPN Annie went walking by, she saw Ellen reaching for her behind, wiping herself with her bare hand. Annie's priorities had just changed.

Meanwhile, John sat back in his upright chair in the lounge and fell asleep watching a 1940s movie on the big screen TV. Dinner was still a few hours away.

We still received regular telephone calls from the charge nurse on duty at Islington House telling us that John fell despite their best efforts, or that John rolled out of bed onto the floor. The last such call came from LPN Penny telling us that John had slipped out of his straight back chair in the lounge. When they got to him he had simply folded his arms, crossed his legs, and started to take a nap on the lounge floor. He told Penny he was "just relaxing, looking around at the ceiling."

I had to smile. Ever since I'd known him, John was one of the most relaxed men I know.

And so go the days in *their world*—coping with longevity.

John and Mary in 1990

"You'd better make friends with Time, because sooner or later it will catch up with you."

- Eleanor Brownn, an internationally recognized inspirational writer.

———∞———

"Let Fate do her worst, there are relics of joy, Bright dreams of the past, which she cannot destroy; — You may break, you may shatter the vase, if you will, But the scent of the roses will hang round it still"

- Thomas Moore (1779 - 1852), Irish poet, singer, and songwriter

Parting Thoughts

John (the Music Man Wannabe)

"I cannot sing the old songs, For visions come again, Of golden dreams departed, And years of weary pain; Perhaps when earthly fetters, shall have set my spirit free, My voice may know the old songs, For all eternity" - The last verse of *"I Cannot Sing the Old Songs,"* written in 1868 by Claribel, the pen name of Charlotte Alington Barnard, a British songwriter and poet.

John, the music man wannabe (Chapter 2), probably never heard this song, but I know that he would like it a lot. If he listened to it, he'd say, "Pow! She hit this one right outa the park!" I know that when the day comes, he'll be singing "Where Are Those Days of My Youth" into eternity.

The Staff Share Their Thoughts

I purposely waited until after I had written this book to ask several of those I dedicated the book to (the staff at the nursing home), if any of them would be willing to share several sentences with me about dementia or Alzheimer's in general, or even a thought about John. What follows are those thoughts, alphabetically arranged by the contributor's last name.

Working with and loving people who are stricken with dementia/Alzheimer's has taught me that while the person in front of me isn't the same person that the family in the room with me knows anymore; that person still recognizes love, and needs to feel loved every day, just like you or I. I have also watched some people who were, by family accounts, very prim and proper and perhaps controlling of their environment, become exactly the opposite! They are very casual and relaxed, laughing and sometimes joking with other residents and staff. Family members marvel about how "different" Mom or Dad is now; and when it's a good change, it's easier to accept. When the change is negative, it's extremely hard for families to wrap their heads around it. It compounds the sadness they already feel when watching someone they love just drift away. I remember when John first came to us, and one thing has never changed; he still flashes those sparkling blue eyes at us, with that devilish grin, and it melts my heart every time! You thank us, and we thank YOU, for trusting us with someone so special. It is an honor to be trusted with the care of our residents and we take that responsibility seriously. I hope many, many people get to read this book and get a better understanding of just how complex this disease is, and how it affects everyone around the person afflicted. - **Shileen Jackson, LPN**

"In my years of caring for the elderly, both with and without Alzheimer's, I have learned: Take the best friend approach, which has allowed me to love and respect them and to appreciate who they are now, their past and what they contributed to society. For that, we both benefit as well as the family. To go home every day knowing you encouraged them into something they enjoyed, made them smile, made a positive connection with them, is what makes life and the ride worthwhile." - **Ellie Johnson, Activity Coordinator**

"John has a good sense of humor. He always says, "Boo" to me when I walk past him. I can just tell by that smirk on his face that he is a joker at heart. I feel it is especially important to keep a sense of humor as we age. He always makes me smile.

It is really rare, and very special, to see couples who have stayed together. Mary and John are one of those couples. I remember when Mary had a very difficult time deciding to leave Islington and move to Westmoor. She just didn't want to leave John. I cannot imagine how difficult that must be.

We have many heartwarming and funny stories to tell. But sometimes it can be heartbreaking to work in long term care. It seems that just as we are getting to know and love our residents they are taken from us.

I feel it is a great honor to be able to partake in end of life care." - **Vicki Ollerenshaw MSW, Director of Social Services**

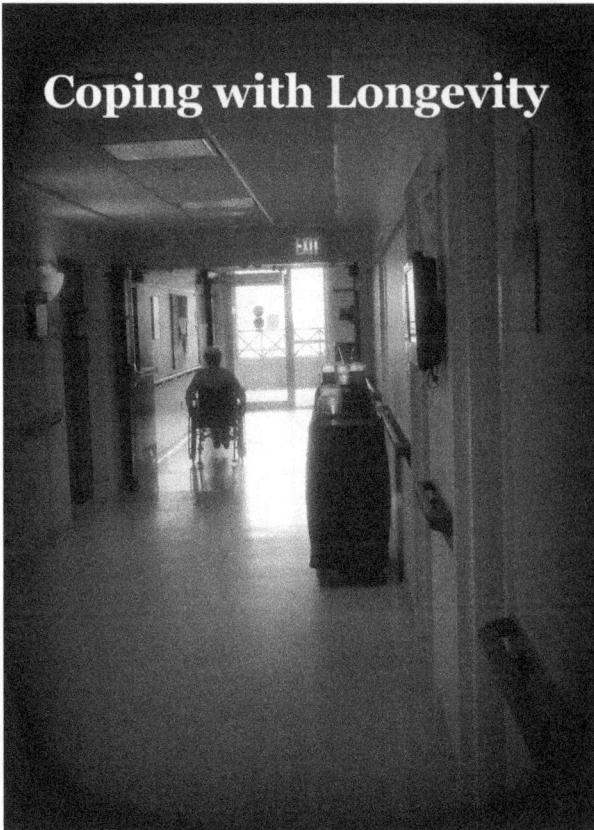

Coping with Longevity

CPSIA information can be obtained
at www.ICGtesting.com
Printed in the USA
BVHW042326031222
653396BV00006B/246

9 781478 787211